Praise for **7 Steps to Raising a Bilingual Child**

"A great resource for parents who want their children to grow up bilingual. *7 Steps to Raising a Bilingual Child* uses clear, accessible prose to present research-based information that debunks the myths associated with learning two or more languages from birth. If you have thought about raising bilingual children but find the prospect daunting, reading this book is an excellent first step in assuaging your fears and in turning the possibility into reality."

—Graciela Vidal, Editor, *Scholastic News, English/Español*

"*7 Steps to Raising a Bilingual Child* makes a very compelling case for the great benefits that come from knowing a second language. It's an invaluable tool for parents who want to expose their children to a second language. The straightforward and informative writing style breaks down the process into small steps that make the goal of raising bilingual children seem completely attainable and, of course, absolutely worthwhile."

—Federica Della Noce, parent raising two bilingual children

"In my line of work, you quickly learn the importance of being multilingual, and we know it will only be more important for the next generation. Insightful and easy-to-digest, *7 Steps to Raising a Bilingual Child* demystifies a complicated issue, dispenses with the common fallacies, and offers easy-to-follow strategies. I heartily recommend it to parents and teachers alike."

—Erik Church, President, EF Institute for Cultural Exchange

"As a bilingual educator who has been involved in the field for over 30 years, I am thrilled finally to see a book specifically addressing the needs and questions of parents who want to raise bilingual children. Dr. Steiner combines solid research in second-language acquisition with practical 'how-to' steps to guide and support families. She dispels the myths surrounding bilingualism and offers sound advice. This book provides sensible and much needed guidance on this topic. Bravo Dr. Steiner!"

—Susan McGilvray-Rivet, Ph.D., Director of ESL, Bilingual and Sheltered English Programs, Framingham Public Schools

W9-BNX-328

7 Steps to Raising a
BILINGUAL CHILD

7 Steps to Raising a
BILINGUAL CHILD

Naomi Steiner, M.D.
with Susan L. Hayes

Foreword by Steven Parker, M.D.

AMACOM
American Management Association

New York | Atlanta | Brussels | Chicago | Mexico City
San Francisco | Shanghai | Tokyo | Washington, D. C.

Special discounts on bulk quantities of AMACOM books are available to corporations, professional associations, and other organizations. For details, contact Special Sales Department, AMACOM, a division of American Management Association, 1601 Broadway, New York, NY 10019. Tel: 212-903-8316.
Fax: 212-903-8083.
E-mail: specialsls@amanet.org
Website: www.amacombooks.org/go/specialsales
To view all AMACOM titles go to: www.amacombooks.org

This publication is designed to provide accurate and authoritative information in regard to the subject matter covered. It is sold with the understanding that the publisher is not engaged in rendering legal, accounting, or other professional service. If legal advice or other expert assistance is required, the services of a competent professional person should be sought.

Library of Congress Cataloging-in-Publication Data

Steiner, Naomi, 1966–
    7 steps to raising a bilingual child / by Naomi Steiner with Susan L. Hayes ; foreword by Steven Parker.
        p.   cm.
    Includes bibliographical references and index.
    ISBN 978-0-8144-0046-3
    1. Bilingualism in children.   2. Child rearing.   3. Child development.   4. Language acquisition.   I. Hayes, Susan L., 1966–   II. Parker, Steven, 1947–   III. Title.   IV. Title: Seven steps to raising a bilingual child.

P115.2.S74   2008
404'.2083—dc22   2008021000

Printing number

10 9 8 7 6 5 4 3 2

CONTENTS

Foreword   xi
Introduction   xv

STEP 1
Building the Foundation for Your Child's Bilingualism   1

What Does It Mean to Be a Bilingual Family?   1
What Does It Mean to Be Bilingual?   2
7 Common Myths about Bilingualism   4
The Bilingual Advantage   19

STEP 2
Making It Happen: Defining Your Goals   25

Decide Which Languages Are Important to You and Why   27
Identify Your Motivations for—and Your Reservations
   about—Bilingualism   28

WORKSHEET 1 Language Questionnaire   29

Choose Which Language(s) You and Your Partner Are Going to
Speak to Your Child 32

Set a Start Date 40

Determine How Proficient You Hope Your Child Will Be in a
Second Language 44

Do a Reality Check. Are Your Proficiency Goals Realistic for
Your Family? 46

Take into Account That One Language Will Be Dominant 47

WORKSHEET 2 My Bilingual Goals and Choices 49

STEP 3

Becoming a Bilingual Coach 51

Part One: Taking Charge 51

Part Two: Who Speaks Which Language When? 56

STEP 4

Creating Your Bilingual Action Plan 65

Part One: Maximizing Language Input at Home 66

Part Two: Making The Most of Community and
Family Resources 74

Part Three: Finding School Support 78

Part Four: How Three Families Are Raising
Bilingual Children 84

Part Five: Create Your Own Bilingual Action Plan 93

WORKSHEET 3 What Are the Key Components to My Bilingual
Action Plan? 94

WORKSHEET 4 Our Family's Weekly Bilingual Schedule 97

STEP 5
Leaping over Predictable Obstacles   99

Predictable Obstacle 1: I'm Not Sure That I'm Speaking to My
Child in a Way That Will Help Him Become Bilingual   100
Predictable Obstacle 2: My Child Does Not Want to Speak My
Language Anymore—She Only Wants to Speak English   107
Predictable Obstacle 3: My Child Keeps Mixing Languages   113
Predictable Obstacle 4: I'm Self-Conscious about Speaking My
Language to My Child in Public   119
Predictable Obstacle 5: Because I'm the One Who Speaks a Second
Language, I Feel Like I'm the One Doing All the Work to Raise
Our Child Bilingual   122
Predictable Obstacle 6: My Work Schedule Has Become Really
Hectic, and There's Little Time for My Child's Bilingualism   125

STEP 6
The "Two Rs": Reading and Writing
in Two Languages   129

Reading in a Second Language   129
The Write Stuff   141

STEP 7
Adapting to School: The Bilingual Child
Goes to School   153

Part One: Public Bilingual Education Programs: Where We've Been,
Where We're at, and Where We're Going   155
Part Two: Results May Vary: How to Handle Special Situations That
Can Affect Your Child's Bilingual Academic Progress   163

Conclusion   171
Bilingual Resource List   175
References   183
Index   191

FOREWORD

I n 1995, a brilliant young pediatrician named Naomi Steiner came to our Division of Developmental and Behavioral Pediatrics at Boston University to do a fellowship. Of course, we were all struck by her impeccable English accent (sure to make anyone sound like a genius, no matter what they say). But Naomi—who grew up in Switzerland—spoke mellifluous French, imposing German, and, in a pinch, some Italian. We hopelessly monolingual professionals were in awe.

We saw first hand how her command of languages was a boon to her professional work. She could converse easily with our many Haitian families and read scientific articles in their original German. It was a skill we all envied.

Over the last decade we have learned a lot more about the advantages of growing up multilingual. Indeed, I now believe that promoting bilingualism is one of the best things a parent can do for his or her 21st-century child. Here's why:

1. Knowing a second language will be a huge advantage in competing for and succeeding in jobs in our ever-shrinking, flat world.

2. Knowing a second language provides a more complex understanding of other countries and cultures.
3. There is evidence that learning a second language early in life confers other advantages for brain development:
   - more cognitive firepower is devoted to language
   - a better ability to deal with distractions
   - easier to learn a 3rd language
   - improved attentional and spatial abilities in the elderly
   - improved memory
   - more creative use of language.

And, best of all, there is zero potential downside. Your grandmother's myths (such as, "bilingualism confuses kids," "bilingualism causes language delays") were wrong. Plus, you don't need to be a superstar to become bilingual. Pretty much any child without a language disability can do so with ease. And the sooner the process begins, while the language acquisition areas of the brain are crackling, the better.

Of course, raising a bilingual child is easier if English is not your primary language. You can and should just speak your native tongue at home from the start. Don't worry, between peers and school and the media, your child will learn accent-free English just fine.

But it's not so easy if you, like most of us hopeless Americans, are a monoglot (the wonderful term for a single language speaker that vaguely sounds like an insult). Here's what won't work: having a foreign nanny for a few years or teaching sign language at 9 months without continuing your child's immersion in that language. You'll have to pick a language to which your child can continue to be exposed (hopefully for at least 5 hours/week), the earlier the better, for many years.

How to achieve this laudable goal in child rearing? Naomi Steiner is clearly the right person at the right time to guide you through every step of this important endeavor. I predict her book will become a classic of its kind. I for one will be recommending it to all my patients and friends. It's thoughtful, wise, well-written, and sympathetic in tone, written by someone who has been there and who has the professional and personal experience and smarts to put it all together for the rest of us.

So, *gracias, merci, vielen Dank* to Dr. Steiner for providing parents with a guidebook on how to raise a multilingual child. It's the right book at the right time by the right person.

Steven Parker, M.D.
Associate Professor of Pediatrics,
Boston University School of Medicine
Division of Developmental and Behavioral Pediatrics,
Boston Medical Center

INTRODUCTION

People are often amazed when my children switch from speaking English with them to talking to my husband in Italian, and then go off to converse in German with their grandmother. "How can your kids be so comfortable speaking more than one language?" they ask.

"They live in an environment where more than one language is spoken," I answer. "So that is what they've learned to do." This is true enough—but it's only the tip of the iceberg.

The rest of the iceberg is vast indeed. Deciding to raise children who speak more than one language is like many other parenting decisions: You start off by gathering information from friends, experts, authors of books and magazine articles, and the Internet. Then, you make the best decision for your family and develop a plan to carry it out.

I first began considering the possibility of raising my children to be bilingual when I was pregnant with my oldest child. Although I was born in England, I grew up speaking four languages. My Swiss husband spoke five. How many languages, I wondered, could our baby learn?

As a developmental and behavioral pediatrician now living in the United States, I was initially confident that I could find the information I needed to make educated choices about raising my children to be bilingual, or even multilingual. After all, in the busy Boston hospital where I practice medicine, I have easy access to speech and language therapists, education specialists, child psychologists, and the most current research studies available.

However, I soon realized that there were enormously conflicting opinions. While some experts were certainly encouraging about raising bilingual children, others cautioned me "not to confuse my child." In other words, I received the same mixed messages about bilingualism that my patients did!

This was more than a little surprising to me, since nearly 20 percent of the children in the United States are currently being brought up to be bilingual, and most parents—like me—have a gut feeling that teaching their child a second language is the right thing to do. As a result, I decided to explore the topic of raising bilingual children more fully. I have spent the past decade conducting my own research on the subject, as my children are growing and are learning multiple languages and as I have continued working with many families who are on the same journey.

In this book, I will take you on a journey of discovery, and I'd like to begin by telling a little bit about my own family's journey. Be assured that my husband and I initially experienced some of the same trepidations that you might be feeling right now, not the least of which was "can we really pull this off?" But we cast away our fears and decided that my husband would speak to our children in Italian and I would speak to them in English. (This is called the One-Parent-One-Language method, which is explained in detail in Step 3.) Even so, my husband was unsure that he could speak to our kids *only* in Italian. Perhaps like you, he was not surrounded by family members who spoke the language, and he was not even speaking it himself on a daily basis. But I hope you'll take heart from our experience. We were both surprised how fast he got into the groove, and how much he enjoyed it. Our children are now 11 and 9, and Italian is the only language that they speak with their dad. What's been really wonderful for me to see is that by sharing a language not spoken by everyone else around them, they've developed a bond that goes so much deeper than simply using words to communicate. When our family returns to the village where my husband grew up, it's as though the children are proudly going back to where they come from too.

I speak only English to the children, and continued to do so even when we lived for a few years in a non-English speaking country. My husband and I speak French to each other, and it has been fascinating to observe the effect this has on our children. One evening when my son was only a toddler, my husband said to me in French, "He looks tired. I think he needs to go to bed," to which our son immediately answered back in English, "I'm not tired!" No secret language for us, I'm afraid! Both our children understand and can speak some elementary French sentences. (I will speak more about this phenomenon of passively learning a language in Steps 1 and 2.)

One thing I learned early on from my research and personal experience, however, is that people feel very strongly about bilingualism, no matter what their own background. The languages we speak have a huge impact on our personal and political identities. Multiple myths—which I discuss in the first chapter—about bilingualism continue to propagate various concerns regarding the adverse effects of raising children to speak more than one language. Even the pediatric residents I teach at the medical center where I work are surprised to hear that bilingualism is not only natural—the majority of people around the world are bilingual—but that it is a fabulous stimulation for a child's developing brain.

Here's another thing that might surprise you: Parents do not have to be bilingual themselves to raise a bilingual child. I'd like to take a moment here to specifically address monolingual parents. If you are monolingual, you can still raise your children to be bilingual!

The step-by-step approach described in this book will work for you, too.

Fortunately, new advances in psycholinguistics and brain research have made it easier to bust these and other negative myths about bilingualism. We can now safely say that there is no scientific evidence to support the idea that giving up one language necessarily promotes the development of another. A child who stops speaking Spanish or Russian, for instance, will not become a better English speaker simply because he focuses his attention on one language.

In this book I will share with you the information I began gathering from professionals and research studies when I was an expectant mother and that I continue to gather today, many years later. Out of this information and my own experience, I have developed a step-by-step approach that will take you from thinking about raising a bilingual child to developing and carrying out a plan for making it happen to overcoming the challenges that can accompany raising a bilingual child. There are a total of seven steps, and each step is one chapter in this book.

In the same way that building a house atop a foundation makes it stronger, having a foundation for raising your child bilingual can make the process easier and go more smoothly. That foundation is understanding bilingualism. I have seen many dedicated parents fail in their effort simply because they did not know the basic facts about bilingualism. Moreover, having this understanding will not only help you teach your child to speak more than one language, it will help you weather the challenges that are inevitably part of the journey and stand firm in your conviction that this was the right decision for you and your child. I help you build the foundation for raising your child bilingual in the first chapter of this book.

The second logical step is to define your bilingual goals. Each parent can have different expectations of what their goals are for their children. Even the definition of bilingualism isn't as obvious as you might think. Just the other day, a pediatrician I work with was surprised to hear that she was bilingual. She can speak some Korean and reads the Korean alphabet, but has difficulty making out the words, so she has never defined herself as "bilingual."

Once you define your bilingual goals, the next two steps are to become comfortable in your role as a bilingual coach and to create a workable Bilingual Action Plan that will allow you to turn your goals into reality. Steps 3 and 4 are critical because children don't just automatically pick up languages. Consistent language input is key, and as you'll see, explicitly defined roles and activities are the key to consistency. Worksheets at the end of Step 4 will help you identify the different bilingual enrichment areas that you want to draw from and create your Bilingual Action Plan. I'll offer examples from other bilingual families that will give you new ideas for supporting a rich bilingual family environment. (You will also find a handy Resource List at the back of the book that you can easily refer to again and again.)

Life, of course, doesn't always go along as expected. In Step 5, I'll present the most predictable hurdles bilingual families face as their children grow and provide strategies for conquering them. What do you do, for instance, when your kindergartner, who has been learning Spanish and English since birth, suddenly insists on speaking only English and pretends not to understand when spoken to in Spanish?

In Step 6, I will explain learning to read and write in a second language. In this "hands-on" chapter, I'll offer concrete examples and activities, illustrating, for example, how to read to your child in a second language.

Finally, there is the academic side of learning languages. In the seventh and final step, I offer a window into the academic lives of bilingual children from preschool through high school. Depending on their personalities, language abilities, and environments, bilingual children take different approaches to school. Some children leap into a bilingual preschool as if it were just another adventure, whereas others initially withdraw and refuse to speak at all in another language. I have observed children learning to read in two different languages without difficulty, while for others, battling two different phonetic systems can simply be too much. If your child struggles with bilingualism in preschool or school, I'll show you how to keep your child's bilingual abilities alive, so that she still feels comfortable with her second or third language.

But as I emphasize at the end of Step 7, the key to raising a bilingual child is to be flexible even when special circumstances crop up to revise your Action Plan, so that your child never has to give up her second language. Along the road to raising a bilingual child, you will—like most parents—sometimes suffer doubts and setbacks. Raj, a freshly graduated college student, recently told me that he was quite fluent in Hindi until high school. Then, as part of his teenage rebellion, he stopped speaking Hindi entirely. Now, nearly 10 years later, he has lost most of his heritage language. Raj says he can now speak Hindi only haltingly and truly regrets that he's not as proficient in the language as he was before. Unfortunately, that is the hard reality of how the brain works: If a language is not used, the brain loses the ability to speak it on command and moves on to perfecting other skills, such as writing essays or learning algebra. But the good news is if a person has at least some active understanding or speaking skills in a language, as Raj does, he can use them as a trampoline to regain his skills in that language fairly rapidly, once he puts in the time and effort.

But the truth is, if Raj's family had reassessed its goals and continued to support his bilingual environment even in the face of his rebellion, he might not have had such a setback at all. The surest way to successfully raise bilingual children is to remain flexible enough to find new ways to support and enrich your family's bilingual environment as your children's needs change. This book will help you both remain true to your bilingual goals and achieve that needed flexibility.

One final note: In my work as a developmental pediatrician, I have yet to meet a parent who regretted raising her child to be bilingual. However, I have heard many, many stories of regret from parents who did not make this choice. My hope in writing this concise, pragmatic, step-by-step book is that you will use it as a guide for offering your children the gift of speaking more than one language.

Building the Foundation for Your Child's Bilingualism

What Does It Mean to Be a Bilingual Family?

If you bought this book, or even if you were casually browsing in your local bookstore and paused to glance through these pages, then you've already taken the first step toward raising a bilingual child and becoming a bilingual family.

Perhaps, like Cecilia, your native language is Spanish, but you can't bring yourself to speak it with your daughter because "it just doesn't come out." Besides, your husband speaks only English, and he tells you that speaking Spanish will only mix up your daughter as she enters kindergarten. Yet, you long to have your daughter carry on the cultural traditions of your family.

Or you might be like Emily, who was raised in the United States but always wanted to learn Italian because she loves opera. She took Italian in college, finally, and traveled to Italy her senior year. Now she's back in the United States and married with two toddlers. She wishes she could introduce her children to the beauty of the Italian language.

You might have picked up this book because you're in a situation similar to Donald's. As a marketing manager, Donald travels so frequently to Japan for his software company that he's taking night classes in Japanese. Now that he realizes how useful it is to speak Japanese with clients, he would like to teach Japanese to his teenagers and boost their understanding of different cultures and career possibilities.

No matter who you are—or what your reasons are for wanting to raise your children bilingual—perhaps you have stopped short of taking that leap because of your own doubts about how to go about it. That's only natural, because thinking about bilingualism can be pretty confusing at times. There seem to be more questions than answers. What is the right age to teach a child another language? Do children who speak more than one language get mixed up between them? How can bilingual children in the United States find a rich enough environment to maintain two languages? How can you possibly start speaking a second language at home if you're not fluent in that language and even your own mother thinks it's a terrible idea to "mix up your kids?"

As a developmental and behavioral pediatrician who has worked for more than a decade with bilingual families in a major urban medical center, I have been fortunate to hear the stories of bilingual families in varied situations. As I mentioned in the introduction to this book, I have yet to meet a family whose members, looking back, wish they *hadn't* raised their children with a second language. On the contrary: Most families soon discover that being bilingual enriches their children's lives—and their own.

What Does It Mean to Be Bilingual?

Now, let's stop here a moment and consider the word "bilingual." What does it really mean? It's a word that few people define in exactly the same way.

2

Is a child bilingual if he understands a language, but won't speak it? Is a child bilingual if he shows much greater proficiency in one language than the other? In other words, does a bilingual child have to listen, speak, read, and write equally well in two languages to count himself bilingual?

The truth is that there are very few "balanced bilinguals"—people who are equally proficient in two languages. Most bilinguals are more comfortable using one language than the other. For the purposes of this book, we're going to use the most inclusive definition of bilingualism possible: the ability to speak, read, write, *or even understand* more than one language. However, chances are, you'll want your child to have a more in-depth knowledge of his second language than simply being able to understand a few words.

The extent of a bilingual child's disparity in fluency depends on that child's unique bilingual environment, which is comprised of the languages spoken by his parents, the languages of his extended family and culture, the language of his community, and the language he hears and uses in school. What's more, your child will soon learn that each language she knows serves a different purpose in her life. Because a child's brain is so adaptable to her needs, the balance between her two languages may shift if she is placed in different circumstances: a new country, a new school, visiting relatives, or even, later on, her career.

The bottom line is that the degree of success you have in raising your child to be bilingual will be directly related to your own family's definition of bilingualism and to your conviction that pursuing that level of language proficiency is the right thing to do. For those reasons, I've presented the seven most common negative myths about bilingualism here—along with scientifically based facts to contradict those myths—followed by a discussion of the many advantages enjoyed by bilingual children and their families. By the end of this chapter, I hope there will be little doubt in your mind that bilingualism is truly a wonderful gift to give your child.

7 Common Myths about Bilingualism

Myth 1: Only really intelligent children can be bilingual.

Fact: Every child can learn multiple languages from birth.

Around the world, people have always instinctively done what you're thinking about doing now: They have taught their children to navigate comfortably in more than one language. Sometimes this happens simply because these families live in countries where more than one language is routinely spoken. Recently, I took a shuttle bus to the airport, and the driver heard me speaking on my cell phone in French and greeted me with a *"bonjour."* This young man explained that he had spent his childhood in Algeria and now speaks four languages. In Algeria, the official language is modern standard Arabic, but Algerians speak to each other in Darja, a North African dialect. In addition, French is taught in the schools, and the majority of Algerian newspapers are in French; to this mix, the young man added English, which he learned to speak fluently after coming to the United States when he was 17.

In Holland, the language is Dutch, which sounds a bit like German, but only the Dutch understand it. So the Dutch need another language for doing business around the world, and therefore their children learn English in school. In Spain, meanwhile, the official language is Spanish, but in the northern part of the country you might also learn Catalan or Basque, depending on your hometown and do business with the rest of the world in English, French, and German. Even in the United States, a country most people think of as strictly English speaking, nearly 20 percent of children 5 years of age and older grow up speaking a language other than English at home.

How is it possible for people to speak so many languages?

Nature made us that way. Through recent studies, we now know that an infant's brain is prewired to learn all of the different languages in the world. That means that, a baby born in Guatemala, for

4

example, can learn Swedish without an accent—if he hears it early on. The brain is made so that babies and children can become bilingual. In fact, some linguists believe children can learn as many as seven different languages without getting confused.

Even newborns can distinguish between the subtle sounds of different languages; in fact, they show a preference for their native languages within four days of life. In one study, for instance, Russian babies sucked harder on their pacifiers when they heard Russian than they did when they heard French. While interpreting behavioral observation in infant studies is difficult and complex, the researchers believe that the intensified sucking meant the babies preferred the sound of their native language. Other experts have discovered that languages as distinct as Hindi, Spanish, and Zulu are easily recognized as being different by infants raised in English-speaking homes.

Of course, how easily any child learns a second language depends on a great many factors, including age, environment, and innate language ability. To some degree, your child's ability to learn different languages is genetic; some individuals really are more gifted at language learning, just as some people are better at math, music, science, or painting. But in the same way that you don't have to be a math genius to become competent at math and you don't have to be a natural musician to learn how to play an instrument, you don't have to be linguistically gifted to learn how to speak more than one language. Remember it is the way that the brain is wired. Additionally, while innate talent is certainly a bonus when it comes to language learning, motivation, instruction, and practice can carry you quite far when it comes to learning anything, languages included.

Also, realize that your child's dominant language can shift if circumstances demand it. The important thing to remember is that a child's brain is extremely adaptable—what scientists call "plastic"—and is wired for survival. No matter how naturally gifted your child is in languages, stimulation will be key to ramping up his proficiency, since fluency in any language is directly proportional to what we read, hear, and speak. That's why in Step 4 I explore in detail numerous different strategies for offering your children language stimulation.

Myth 2: **Bilingualism leads to confusion, causing children to mix languages and never become proficient in either.**

Fact: **It is normal for children to mix languages as they learn them.**

As I explained earlier, it is rare for bilingual children (or adults, for that matter) to exhibit equal proficiency in both languages. Balanced bilinguals are the exception, not the rule; not surprisingly, most children expand on the language that they hear and use the most and that becomes their dominant language.

One of the many misconceptions about bilingualism is that the ability to think and speak in a second language automatically guarantees proficiency on demand in that language—even when one is in the process of learning the language. There's also the expectation that a person who is bilingual will *always* be able to find just the right words in both languages (something that monolinguals aren't able to do all the time in their single language!). Such misconceptions and false expectations can lead people to believe, erroneously, that whenever a bilingual speaker mixes languages he must be "confused" about which language he's speaking.

Let me be clear: Young bilingual children *often* mix both languages as they speak. This is part of the natural course of learning two languages. Yet monolinguals often find this mixing of languages disturbing, and even educators sometimes misinterpret this natural process as a sign that the child is "confused" about which language he is speaking and what he wants to say. This is often seen—incorrectly— as proof that bilingualism leads to poor proficiency in both languages.

To date, researchers still haven't determined exactly how children learn more than one language. Is a baby aware that she's learning two separate languages? Does the brain put all of the language information in one place, or are the words of both languages placed into completely separate brain "compartments" from the get-go? For instance, if a baby hears Portuguese from one parent and English from another, are both languages stored in one part of the brain at the start, then identified as distinct entities and separated later in life? If this is the case, that could explain why some bilingual children mix their languages initially.

To children, of course, none of this matters. They just do what they need to do. If 2-year-old Juan, born in the United States to an American mother and a Peruvian father, asks his Spanish-speaking grandmother for his shoes so that he can play outside, he may say the sentence in Spanish, but forget that "shoes" is "*zapatos,*" in which case he'll likely substitute the English word within the Spanish sentence: "*Abuela, yo quiero mis* shoes *para jugar afuera.*"

Does Juan know that he's producing a sentence where one language interferes with another? Perhaps. Does he care? Most likely not, as long as his grandmother helps him find his sneakers so he can get out the door! In other words, his main goal is to communicate his wants and needs.

Questions about language acquisition are incredibly complex for researchers to study and answer, because the child's brain is developing as he's learning languages—and the very act of learning languages can impact how the brain develops. We do know, however, that by 3 years of age most children are aware that they are speaking different languages when they switch between them and can identify each language. They might even label a certain language as "Daddy's language" or "Nana's language" and can translate simple words.

As their brains continue to mature, bilingual children typically become more efficient at separating languages. Certain children will mix languages a lot during this maturation process, while others will do it only briefly or not at all. The natural process of separating languages can last until mid-childhood, and different children mix their languages in various ways. For instance, some bilingual children may initially use the grammar rules from one language and the vocabulary from a different language, such as adding the English "-ing" to the end of a verb in another language, while others apply the same grammar rules to both languages. It's common, too, for bilingual children to create compound words out of two separate words from two separate languages or to switch from one language to another while speaking.

Often, a child's environment will influence how he mixes languages or the circumstances under which he switches between them. For instance, a child who usually speaks French to one parent might slip out of that language and include English expressions within the same sentence: "*Dépêches-toi, Papa* (Hurry up, Daddy), baseball practice is about to start, and I'm the first to bat." In this case, the child might be switching into English because he's accustomed to speaking English with his baseball coach and friends.

Of course, children who grow up in families or communities where mixing languages is common will do so more than children growing up in environments where language rules are strictly adhered to in each language. In the United States, Hispanic families often speak a mix of Spanish and English. Centuries ago, Yiddish, which is still used today, evolved out of a combination of German and eastern European languages.

Even adult bilinguals continue to mix their languages at times, and would be amused if someone tried to tell them that they are "confused," so why should children feel differently? For instance, one kindergartner told her mother, "*Je veux aller* (I want to go) swimming now." When I asked the little girl if she was confused about which languages she was speaking, she gave me a surprised look. "Even if I don't know the word in French, I still want to go swimming," she said. That's because language is primarily a tool used to communicate and to be understood.

So, as you listen to your children learn to master different languages, remember that switching from one language to another is just second nature for most bilinguals, especially in the early phases of language learning. As one older bilingual child once said to me, "People who only speak one language just don't know what it feels like in the head to speak two."

Additionally, far from experiencing confusion, bilinguals reap many intellectual advantages that I will discuss in more detail later in this Step.

Myth 3: **If a child doesn't speak English by the time she enters kindergarten, she will have trouble learning to read and have difficulty in school.**

Fact: **A child's brain adapts to her language environment, and a child can learn a language well beyond 5 years of age.**

When it comes to learning languages, experts generally agree that earlier is better. A baby's brain is prewired to learn multiple languages. During the second part of a baby's first year of life, the infant's brain shifts. He begins concentrating on the languages he's exposed to, as the nerve pathways in the brain start to consolidate and specialize. Once that specialization begins, a baby starts to lose his ability to absorb the sounds of languages that he's not exposed to frequently.

But this dimming of a child's inherent ability to learn different languages doesn't happen overnight. In fact, experts believe that the ability to learn multiple languages declines slowly until puberty. At that point, becoming bilingual is a rockier journey for most people; languages learned after puberty are not "mother tongues" any more. Recently, researchers have done studies that look at which parts of the brain are activated when a person speaks a second language.

9

Some studies suggest that when people speak a language learned later in life, a different part of the brain is activated than when they speak their first language. Even though this finding is complex and still debated, it leads us to question whether learning a language later in life might be a somewhat distinct learning process from becoming bilingual during infancy and early childhood.

Interestingly, other researchers have found that if a person has a high level of proficiency in the second language, then the area of activation in the brain overlaps that of the first language. In beginner speakers, on the other hand, the "activation site" of the second language may be situated farther away from that of the more proficient first language. In some cases, the activation may even spill over into the opposite side of the brain from where the language area is typically located. To make things even more fascinating (and murky), these results can vary enormously from one person to another.

But in any case, it is safe to say that individuals who learn a second language during adolescence or adulthood may have to make more of an effort to become fluent in that language than those who learn one as children. Also, there's a good chance that people who learn a language after puberty will speak that language with an accent.

What do these theories about language acquisition mean for your family? Obviously, the earlier you start raising your children to be bilingual, the more successful you're likely to be. But you certainly needn't abandon the idea of having a bilingual family if your children are already past the widest window of bilingual opportunity. There is absolutely no deadline beyond which the human brain fails to learn a new language.

In fact, you can learn another language along with your children, providing a role model as well as guidance in the learning process. For instance, when Anna started speaking to her first newborn in her native Swedish, her husband Frank felt isolated, since he didn't understand a word she said. With the help of a language course, language tapes in the car and, most of all, hearing Anna speak with their children, Frank learned Swedish as his children did.

Frank is proud of his accomplishment, and learning Swedish has helped him to feel closer to Anna and the children. What's more, as we'll see later in this chapter, there are many advantages to becoming bilingual *at any age.*

Myth 4: Bilingualism leads to language delay.

Fact: Children learning two languages sometimes start talking a little later, but no research has shown that bilingualism typically leads to anything more than a temporary language delay.

Misinformation about the negative effects of bilingualism may lead your child's teacher to recommend that your child use only English, particularly if your child doesn't seem to be speaking as well as his peers. Resist this advice!

The reality is that delayed speech or language development is the most common developmental challenge, affecting between 5 and 10 percent of all children, whether they're bilingual or not. Language learning problems are four times more common in boys than girls. These numbers hold true for bilingual kids as well as monolingual kids, and it is imperative to underline the fact that bilingualism is not the cause of language learning difficulties.

Children learn languages in the context of their environments. They will not usually master fully equivalent vocabularies in both languages but will learn and apply words in ways that seem most appropriate. For instance, if a child speaks Polish at home, she will likely learn words pertaining to the home—like pots, pans, pillow, remote control, bedroom, grandmother—in Polish. If she's attending school in English, she'll probably learn school-related words—bus, eraser, blackboard, desk—in English. Then there will be words that she uses in both environments, such as lunch, water, door, and paper. However, because she might not know how to say "broom" in English, this might stand out in the classroom.

Research shows that if you consider *total* vocabulary from both languages, a bilingual child usually knows the same number of words as her monolingual peers. Any small discrepancies wane over time, and typically disappear by kindergarten. After that, a bilingual child may actually end up with *greater* word comprehension than a monolingual child.

There is scant research regarding language milestones for bilingual children, but we do know that they're comparable to a monolingual child's. Any mild delays experienced by a bilingual child are usually in "expressive" language, which means that the bilingual child might have a normal level of language comprehension, but suffers a temporary delay in speaking the language when compared to monolingual children of the same age. Is this because a bilingual child is learning twice the amount of information? Is it a question of memorization capacity? Or could it be because a child hasn't had enough time to practice each language? Nobody knows for sure. What's important is that these language lags usually disappear before 5 years of age.

You should also know that there is a broad range of "normal" for each milestone in language development, even in monolingual children. This spectrum can be striking: For instance, some monolingual toddlers start talking profusely by 18 months, while others only begin putting two words together in their first shaky sentences at around 24 months. In fact, at 18 months, only about 10 percent of monolingual toddlers combine words into sentences, whereas by 2 years of age, only 10 percent *do not* combine words to form sentences. These substantial variations are also present among bilingual children, but parents and educators often leap to the conclusion that it is *because* a child is learning two languages that her learning is delayed.

While there's no evidence that suggests bilingualism can be the cause of a significant language delay, language and developmental delays can impact your approach to your child's bilingualism. I explore this topic in depth in Step 7.

Unfortunately, when faced with a bilingual child who seems to be struggling with language acquisition, educators may focus on what's happening only in the classroom rather than look at a child in the context of his whole environment. To prevent misleading recommendations, it's important for you to be informed and to remind your children's teachers that bilingual children learn languages differently from their monolingual peers. Comparing the two groups is not helpful. The all-too-common advice doled out by professionals, such as speech and language therapists, educators, and pediatricians, is to limit your child's exposure to *just one language.* They continue to offer this advice even though there is absolutely no scientific evidence that dropping one language spurs development in another. In fact, the very opposite is true: Being forced to give up one language can be very disturbing for children emotionally, especially if that child uses, or even worse, is dependent on, that particular language to communicate with certain beloved individuals.

Of course, if you're at all concerned about your child's language development, you should not hesitate to bring this up with your pediatrician. It's important to have your child be assessed by a speech and language therapist—ideally one who knows that your child is being raised bilingual. The gold standard is assessment in both languages, but if that's not possible, at least try to see a therapist who is experienced in dealing with bilingual children. You should know that in a study of children who failed developmental screening tests, such as those done at your pediatrician's office, 80 percent had parents who were concerned ahead of time about their child's development. So listen to your intuition.

If you have your child evaluated and do discover that your bilingual child has a language or learning delay, there's no need to abandon your goal of having your child speak more than one language; you can simply reassess your Bilingual Action Plan. I'll explain how to do that in the seventh and final Step in this book.

Myth 5: Parents must be fluent in more than one language before raising a bilingual child.

Fact: Monolingual parents can raise a bilingual child.

No matter how many languages you speak, you're probably more comfortable using one language more than another, and you may wonder which language to use when speaking to your child at home. My advice is that each parent should speak the language he or she is most fluent in with their children.

When you speak a language fluently, your child is exposed to a much wider vocabulary and to correct grammar. Language also encompasses expressions, nursery rhymes, songs, story telling, and sayings that have been passed down from one generation to the next. All of these elements represent communication at a sophisticated emotional level, which is important in any language. Speaking in your most fluent language with your children will offer them more expressive, diverse words and phrases and help them develop a full vocabulary and range of expressions.

Now, what if you and your spouse or partner can only speak English? Is it still possible to raise a bilingual child?

Absolutely. There is no evidence at all that a child with English-speaking monolingual parents can't learn a foreign language. Think of the families who move to foreign countries. In those situations, parents and kids all hit the books, and the entire family starts to learn the language. Generally, everyone is surprised at the level of proficiency they can achieve.

Even if you don't have the advantage of living in another country where you're immersed in a second language, it's still possible to

14

raise a bilingual family. You can learn a language as your children do, using all of the bilingual activities and resources I describe in Step 4 of this book, providing a role model for your children as you guide them into the bilingual world.

It's even possible to raise bilingual children without ever learning another language yourself. For instance, at the beginning of Step 2 you'll meet an English-speaking couple in New York City who chose to teach their three daughters Mandarin without themselves knowing a word of it. It all started with the family's first Mandarin-speaking nanny; later all three children participated in advanced Chinese classes in high school and graduated as balanced bilinguals, speaking, reading, and writing comfortably in both languages.

You'll find more information on how monolingual parents can raise a bilingual child specifically in Step 2 as well as throughout the book.

Myth 6: Children absorb a language passively, "like a sponge."

Fact: A child's brain is wired to learn different languages, but adequate language stimulation is a must. A poor language environment can lead to a child becoming a "passive" bilingual.

"Use it or lose it" is a phrase that perfectly summarizes language learning. As I've already discussed, the brain of an infant or young child is like a sponge, readily absorbing and retaining the different sounds of up to seven languages. Yet, that child's brain will soon start specializing in only one language if the environment does not continue to provide stimulation in the second or third, and the child will soon lose his ability to learn and remember more than the one language he is exposed to.

If your child is never schooled in a second language or encouraged to read and speak it, but hears a second language spoken at home, at school, or in his community, he will become quite good at understanding it. However, his spoken, written, and reading fluency will be limited by his lack of active engagement. This is common in the United States, where first generation immigrants so often converse with their children only in English and send them to English-only schools.

Even so, passive bilingualism—the ability to understand a language without speaking it—is a solid first step toward reaping the advantages of bilingualism. In Canada, for instance, passive bilingualism is promoted at the federal level to increase understanding between English- and French-speaking citizens; it's also a requirement for entry into many Canadian colleges or universities. Certainly, passive bilingualism is a gateway to a language and culture, and from there anyone can expand on fluency.

However, in hindsight, many parents often do regret not advocating more active use of a second language. That's why it's important to determine, as early as possible, what your bilingual goals are for your family, and to develop a specific, workable plan for achieving them.

Myth 7: The English language is losing ground in the United States and elsewhere.

Fact: English is far from disappearing. In fact, the English language is expanding rapidly throughout the world.

Many books about bilingualism sidestep any discussion of the English-only focus of public education in the United States. However, the bias against bilingualism is integral to what most parents must deal with if they're interested in raising bilingual children.

The United States has always attracted, and continues to attract, immigrants from around the world. They come for the promise of freedom from religious and political oppression and for the wealth of opportunities this country offers. The unity and survival of people living in the United States has always depended on the ability of immigrants to assimilate into the majority culture and that assimilation has been directly tied to the ability of immigrants to learn English. In the minds of many Americans, English proficiency is tied to our national identity.

Historically, immigrants have been expected to learn English at the expense of their languages of origin; more often than not, by the third generation of an immigrant family, children may not speak or understand the language of their grandparents at all. This is a tremendous loss for everyone concerned.

The impulse to adopt English as the only language has not just been driven by immigrants eager to succeed in the United States, but also by U.S. citizens who fear that immigrants are "taking over" the country. These same citizens balk at the idea of a country where people speak anything other than English; they envision (and fear) an entirely Spanish-speaking New York, for instance, or a San Francisco where Asian languages overcome English. Yet, U.S. Census data shows that most immigrants continue to learn English at a proficient level. Today's immigrants are actually becoming fluent in English faster than in previous decades.

In fact, if you take a look at the expansion of English fluency around the world, it's easy to see that English has a firm foothold in the world of international commerce and technology. One-quarter to one-third of all people in the world understand and speak some English; foreign countries have made and continue to make an impressive effort to teach English at early ages in the schools. There is no rationale for fearing that English will stop being the dominant language in the United States or widely used around the world.

At the same time, many people are now aware that English isn't enough. They want their children to experience other cultures through other languages and view bilingualism as a way to explore the world and deepen one's respect for the many different cultures surrounding their own.

For a comparison of the seven myths, see Table 1.1.

TABLE 1.1

Myths and Facts about Bilingualism

Myths	Facts
If a child is not very intelligent, then he cannot become bilingual.	*A baby's brain is naturally made to learn multiple languages.*
A child will become "confused" and mix languages if he learns more than one language.	*Mixing is a natural step in learning multiple languages.*
If a child does not speak English by kindergarten, she will have difficulty in school and difficulty learning to read.	*A child can adapt and learn languages well beyond 5 years of age.*
Bilingualism leads to language delay.	*There is no scientific research that shows that bilingualism leads to language delay.*
A parent must be fluent in more than one language to raise her child bilingual.	*Monolingual parents can raise their child bilingual.*
Children just absorb a language passively.	*The brain requires a rich and stimulating environment for a person to become a fluent speaker.*
The English language is losing ground in the United States.	*English is far from disappearing in the United States and the world.*

The Bilingual Advantage

No doubt about it: Bilingual kids are off to a brainy head start. Recent research reveals that even children who are far more proficient in one language than the other are better off than children who are exposed to only one language. For example, one study found that children who knew just a little Italian in addition to their native English had a greater understanding of words and more enhanced reading skills than their peers who spoke only English. The authors of the study believe that children gain cognitive and academic benefits even from just a little exposure to a second language.

Language Benefits

Learning another language gets the brain machinery going. The tasks of learning two sets of vocabulary and grammar, then learning how to shift from one language to another, provide terrific brain stimulation. Even better, a bilingual child doesn't just learn a second set of words, but gains the ability to compare and translate languages, making connections between words in both languages and what they symbolize. Thinking about language is a very sophisticated exercise that comes early and naturally to bilingual children.

If you know English and Spanish, for instance, you know that we say a woman "gives birth" to her child in English. In Spanish, she would "*dar luz*," which, literally translated, means "gives light." Knowing these two phrases, you can begin to think of the process of birth in a different way: a woman is not only giving birth, a very physical act, but giving light, which yes, is physical, but also spiritual, in the sense that a new soul is on the planet because of her physical, creative, and spiritual transition to motherhood. Bilinguals are therefore not just learning words, but how to think about the world in more than one way. Bilinguals can become more effective at communicating even the most tenuous, ephemeral ideas.

Academic Benefits

From an academic perspective, your bilingual child will reap many advantages. Around the world, research shows that bilinguals are more creative and detailed when answering exam questions, perhaps because knowing words in different languages offers them more elasticity and flexibility in their thinking. Although many of the more complex words in English have a French root (because in 1066 the Normans from the north of France invaded Britain), English is considered to be a Germanic language. So, many commonly used English words have a German root (see Table 1.2).

So if a child is knowledgeable in a Romance language, such as Spanish, Italian, or French, she can analyze unfamiliar English words and perform better on written exams. This might be why a study of elementary school children in Louisiana found that foreign language study helped boost overall performance for kids, and another study reported that secondary students who studied a foreign language scored higher on college entrance exams like the SATs.

Analytical thinking starts early in a bilingual child, because he has already learned how to break words down into "pieces." Research studies demonstrate that bilinguals have an increased "phonological awareness"—that means they are better able to recognize different sounds within one word. This is particularly important for pre-

TABLE 1.2

German and French Roots in the English Language

English	German	French
Speak	*Sprechen*	Parler
Bilingual	Zweisprachig	*Bilingue*

schoolers and kindergartners, because the first step in learning to read is to learn how to hear and break words down into disparate sounds.

Overall, the rules for learning languages make more sense to a bilingual child than to a child who has heard only one language. For example, a second grader trying to understand the difference between "to," "too," and "two" will have an easier time of it if that child has already learned to juggle words, sounds, and meanings in different languages on a daily basis. Understanding language rules in general can also make learning a third or fourth language easier later on in life.

Other Cognitive Benefits

Instead of thinking that bilingual children suffer cognitive disadvantages, scientists now believe that bilinguals are at least cognitively equal to their monolingual peers. Language plays an enormous role in cognitive development, which is the development of the ability to think and solve problems. For instance, our brain uses language to organize abstract thoughts. Research demonstrates that bilingualism promotes abstract thinking.

It's easy to imagine how the brain of a bilingual child—who is necessarily an expert in comparing and organizing words—can have a head start in thinking about problems and solving them in any arena. Studies have shown that bilingual children grasp rules and process information more easily, even in math!

Why would this be true? Possibly because a bilingual child already has a more flexible brain. Other research suggests that the bilingual brain is better at problem solving, creativity, and memorizing. In fact, a bilingual child who is proficient in two languages may even show a slight superiority over his monolingual classmates in IQ testing. This isn't necessarily because that child is inherently more intelligent, but because he's had more extensive experience in switching between languages, and therefore might be a better problem solver.

Family and Community: Bilingualism as a Bridge Between Cultures

Bilingualism is not only about learning words in two different languages, but about connecting with two different cultures. As a developmental and behavioral pediatrician and also as a mother, I like to look at each child as a whole. Yes, each child is a unique individual. But she also lives in a family and in a community and is a child of the world. Being bilingual gives her better communication skills and a better understanding not only of the world around her, but of the many varied roles she can play in that world.

A child does not live alone and talk to herself. Language is about communication. A child is a member of a family both near and extended, and if members of that family speak more than one language, it stands to reason that the child will have closer emotional bonds to both her family and her culture of origin if she can speak all of her "heritage" languages—the languages of her extended family.

Research has shown that children who are brought up to be bilingual have a sense of where they come from and feel proud of their heritage. These children sometimes describe themselves as being a bridge between cultures. For instance, a 2002 study of U.S. adolescents who were second-generation immigrants showed that those who kept their parents' native languages have better relationships within their families, feel better about themselves, and have a more positive attitude about school than their peers who "lose" their heritage language and become monolingual English-speakers.

Another researcher reports that bilingual children have a sophisticated sense of their identities. They go beyond perceiving themselves as creating a bridge between family members of different languages or cultures to seeing themselves as capable of enhancing acceptance among people of diverse origins around the world. As one teenager put it, "When kids know two languages, it makes them happy to help others."

The truth is, you can probably get by just fine speaking only English. It is, after all, the language of technology and trade. But beyond conferring language, academic, cognitive, and even economic advantages, being able to speak a second language opens up new avenues of cultural understanding and connection for your child within your family, your community, and our world. What I said at the beginning of this chapter bears repeating here: A second language truly is a gift, and it is one that I hope very much you will want to give your child (see Table 1.3 on page 24).

TABLE 1.3

Positive Points about Raising a Bilingual Child

The child	All kids can do it	• Bilingualism is not dependent upon a certain level of intelligence
	Brain stimulation	• Thinking about languages • Comparing languages • Problem solving
The family	All parents can do it	• You don't need to be a superparent • Bilingualism also works if you're monolingual • Interest in others
	Language is communication	• Special child-parent bond
The community	Communication between cultures	• Proud of heritage language • Bridge between generations • Bridge between cultures • Cultural awareness
The world	Globalization	• Opening a child's mind to different facets of the world • "I can get around anywhere with English" is out of date • "I can communicate in different languages" is "in" • Being a citizen of the world

2

Making It Happen: Defining Your Goals

Jennifer and John are native New Yorkers who never spoke a word of any language other than English until they had children. Yet they raised their three daughters to speak both English and fluent Mandarin-Chinese. Yes, Mandarin! On the face of it, everything about this scenario sounds unlikely: monolingual parents and bilingual children, the choice of the second language, and the high level of fluency the children reached in both languages. But it began simply enough. When Jennifer returned to work a few months after the birth of her oldest daughter, she hired a babysitter who spoke Mandarin but hardly any English. "At the time, it never occurred to me that by hiring Mei Feng, I was making a life-altering decision for our daughter and her sisters who were not yet born, as well as for my husband and myself," Jennifer says. But when her daughter started to pick up Mandarin, Jennifer decided to do everything she could to help her, and later her sisters, become bilingual. "I thought, how many kids in America get the chance to learn Chinese?" she says. "It was too good an opportunity to pass up, and besides, our daughters really seemed to enjoy it." Thereafter, Jennifer only hired Mandarin-speaking babysitters, and Mei Feng remained with the family as their Mandarin language tutor.

When the girls reached high school, they were fluent enough to be placed in a class called "Chinese for Native Speakers," and since then, all three have traveled to China on intensive language instruction courses. Even Jennifer herself eventually studied Mandarin for five years—"in self-defense" as she puts it.

Samantha, on the other hand, studied Spanish in high school and college. She developed such a high degree of fluency and love for the language that she became a Spanish teacher. Having achieved bilingualism herself, she knew it was something she wanted for her own children. So when she had kids, she decided to speak to them only in Spanish. When her children reached kindergarten, they were more fluent in Spanish than they were in English. "I had experienced firsthand how difficult it is learn a language, much less become fluent in it, when you don't start until high school," Samantha says. "So I was determined to do it differently with my children. It was amazing how fast they picked up the language."

As you can see, whether you yourself are monolingual or bilingual, the way you go about helping your child become bilingual isn't that much different from the way you'd go about helping him become, say, a highly skilled swimmer or piano player: You provide him with lots of instruction and opportunity to practice, ideally, starting from a young age. And as with any other long-term parenting goals being clear in your own mind why you would like to raise your child bilingual and what you hope your child will gain from being bilingual is an important and, I would argue, an essential, step toward making it happen. It can also make the process easier!

This Step is designed to help you gain that clarity, and as a result, make it possible at the end of the Step for you to readily define your bilingual goals for your child. To achieve that end, I've broken down the Step into a seven item "to-do" list.

1. Decide which languages are important to you and why.
2. Identify your motives for (and your reservations about) bilingualism.

3. Choose which language(s) you and your partner are going to speak to your child. (Here, I also address six frequently asked questions about language choice.)
4. Set a start date.
5. Determine how proficient you hope your child will be in the second language.
6. Do a reality check. Are your proficiency goals realistic for your family?
7. Take into account that one language will be dominant.

Whatever Your Bilingual Goals, Go for Them!

As you read through the items on the to-do list and start to develop your vision, I encourage you to simply go for it. Bilingualism is not as complicated or as overwhelming as it may seem. In fact, on many levels, it's really about one word after another. That's what ultimately leads to the mastery of any language. So don't feel daunted, and don't delay starting. I often tell parents "postponing bilingualism often means never starting bilingualism." And if you never start, you may feel—wrongly—less capable and, perhaps even worse, a sense of regret. Clearly, planning and effort will be required, but I can guarantee you that hearing your child speak her first words in a second language will give you the confidence that you are doing the right thing and encourage you to stick with it. So go ahead, start with that first word.

1. Decide Which Languages Are Important to You and Why

Most Americans can proudly trace their family origins. Likewise, the majority of Americans feel an emotional attachment to one, and in some cases, many other languages, in addition to English. For one person, it may be French, because she studied it in school, for another, Russian, because he heard his *babushka*, or grandmother,

27

speak it. For yet another, it may be Swahili, the language spoken in East Africa, because that's where her ancestors came from.

The "Language Questionnaire" (Worksheet 1) can help you see, at a glance, which languages have special meaning for you, and why. And that, in turn, can help you choose which language you would like your child to learn. Some questions to think about as you fill out the worksheet:

- What are your roots? Where does your family come from originally?
- What do you value about your heritage?
- Which languages do you speak, and how does it make you feel when you speak them?
- Which languages do members of your family speak? Which languages have previous generations spoken?
- Which languages have you been exposed to, and what do you like about them?
- Which languages would you like to speak or would you like your child to speak? Why?

2. Identify Your Motivations for—and Your Reservations about—Bilingualism

If you're monolingual . . .

If you speak a single language but are interested in raising your child to speak an additional one, chances are you're culturally savvy, curious about the world and the different peoples who inhabit it, and appreciative of their languages. Perhaps you or your partner feel a tie to a specific country and its language because of your family, your work, or, like Emily in Step 1 who was inspired to learn Italian because of her love for opera, something you are passionate about.

While the decision to raise a child to be bilingual is an intensely personal one, there are several reasons I hear over and over from

WORKSHEET 1

Language Questionnaire

Which language do you feel an attachment to?	How or why do you feel attached to this language?	Rate from 0–10 how important this language is to you.
Example: Italian	*From my great-grandmother. I heard her speak it when I was a young kid. And she would call me "piccolino."*	*4*
Example: Spanish	*I took it in high school and am quite fluent. My best friend comes from Argentina, and I have visited his family there a few times.*	*7*

monolingual parents. You may find one (or more) of your own reasons reflected here:

- "I don't want my child to think that English is the 'best,' or the only, language that people speak."
- "I believe learning another language will help open my child's eyes to other countries and cultures."
- "Globalization does not only mean the expansion of American culture. It also means there's an increased need to understand other cultures."
- "I never learned another language, and when I travel, I am somewhat embarrassed. The first thing that I have to say when I open my mouth is always 'Do you speak English?' I would love to be able to chat in French with the *boulanger* when I ask for *une baguette, s'il vous plaît.*
- "I believe being able to speak a foreign language could open doors for my child when he is older. It could help him get into college and later, land a good job."

But I find there tends to be one thing, above all others, that holds monolingual parents back from raising their child bilingual: the thought of having to embark down the road of learning the language themselves.

While it's true that a child's young and adaptable brain picks up languages more easily than an adult's brain does, the good news is adults can and do learn languages! And, actually, adults have many skills that give them a distinct advantage over children when it comes to learning a language. You, for example, easily grasp the concept of grammar, such as the use of tenses. Young children have difficulty with that. And your higher cognitive skills and reading ability allow you to pick up a lot more from written language, which means you are not as dependent as kids are on oral practice.

And even if you don't make a conscious decision at the outset to learn the second language that your child is learning, it's never too late to start. After a while, you may find yourself picking up the books like Jennifer, who studied Mandarin, did. The positive impact this can have on your child is enormous. When your child sees you learning and, yes, at times struggling, but ultimately progressing, it sets a powerful example for him—and no less of one than if you were already bilingual.

If you're bilingual . . .

The flip side of the melting pot story is that as diverse peoples come together their differences tend to disappear. Thus, bilingual parents often tell me they feel pulled between two cultures. They recognize the importance of their origins, but they feel completely a part of the mainstream culture. Some say they feel uncomfortable at the thought of speaking a language other than the one predominantly spoken in their country when talking with their children in public, while others, who stopped speaking the language regularly years ago, worry they wouldn't be able to speak it well at all. Sometimes it seems as though bilingual parents can give me as many reasons for *not wanting* their children to speak their native language as monolingual parents can for *wanting* their children to speak a second language! But as I've said before, I've never met a parent who regretted raising his or her child bilingual—even those that may have had some doubts in the beginning.

Alexis was one of those with doubts. His family immigrated to the United States from Russia when he was in elementary school, and he quickly became all too conscious of being different. "I was the Russian kid on the block," he says. "It took me a while to learn English and, until I did, I got kicked around." In part because the bullies became his friends once he learned their language, it didn't really hit Alexis how traumatic the experience had been until two decades later, when his wife was pregnant with their son. That's when Alexis realized how ambivalent he felt about his child learning Russian. On the one hand, Alexis planned to name his son Dmitri, after his own father, and he wanted the boy to be proud of where he came from. But, on the other hand, Alexis didn't want his son to feel different from, much less be bullied by, his peers in the way that he had been years before.

After wrestling with his feelings, Alexis decided shortly before Dmitri's birth that he would teach him Russian, and he's been amazed and delighted at how many of his own happy childhood memories have been awakened as he shares Russian nursery rhymes, songs, folk tales and other traditions with his young son.

Josh didn't doubt that he wanted to pass his language, Hebrew, along to his baby daughter. He just doubted that he'd be able to do it. "I hadn't really spoken Hebrew since high school, and I wasn't sure that I would remember it," he says. "But then a moment came that I will always remember: holding Sarah for the first time in the delivery room and saying *"Shalom chamudi,"* or "hello sweetie" in Hebrew. After that, Josh said, one word just followed another.

3. Choose Which Language(s) You and Your Partner Are Going to Speak to Your Child

For many parents, the choice of language is obvious. For example, if you speak only English and your partner speaks a second language, there's no great dilemma. Yet the situation is not always so clear-cut. Monolingual parents might have different languages in mind that they feel would work for their family. Other parents might speak more than two languages. And if your family moves around internationally, you are exposed to multiple cultures and languages.

So it's not that surprising that the all-important question of "Which language do I choose?" often begets more questions. Here, I've presented—and answered—the six most frequent questions I'm asked regarding language choice.

Six Common Questions about Choosing a Language

1. My language really can't help my child in life. Wouldn't he be better off learning French or German?

Unfortunately, languages are often seen in terms of their "value" or "status." English is an example of a language that has a high value because it's seen as representing education and wealth. French, which historically was the language that nobility and royalty used to speak to one another, also carries a lot of status.

The perceived value of a language has become so ingrained that some people do not even consider what they speak to be a language. For example, when I ask people who have immigrated to the United States from India how many languages they speak, they often answer one (English) or perhaps two (English and Spanish). Then I ask (somewhat incredulously), "Don't you speak any languages from India?" And in an offhand way they will name one or two "local dialects" (their words, not mine), each of which happens to be spoken by millions of people and is extremely different from the other!

But a language—and when I use the word "language" I include all languages and all dialects—is much more than the value given to it by other people. When choosing a language for your child, remember to think about all the ways in which you hope your child will benefit from it. *Any* language has the potential to enhance your child's life, and lead to experiences that would not be possible without it.

Tatiana, for example, speaks Romanian, her native language, to her daughter, Nadia. In the summer, instead of going to camp, Nadia goes to stay with her non-English-speaking grandparents in Romania. This would not be possible if Nadia didn't speak Romanian. She would then miss out on an experience she loves, as well as getting to know her grandparents, their village, and the "*fuarte gustos,*" or "very tasty," foods they eat. So for Nadia and her family, Romanian is an extremely valuable language indeed.

Many children are denied their heritage language simply because others tell their parents that the language is "not going to help them in life" and, therefore, is unimportant. Yet when a child integrates his heritage into his life with pride, it leads to an increase in self-esteem and self-worth. And when parents do not pass along their heritage, they run the risk of their child feeling ashamed of where his family comes from. So, what "helps" a child in life is actually highly subjective and personal and will be different for each family. And certainly, your child's brain does not care about a language's so-called value— the brain benefits no matter what the second language is. But perhaps the most practical argument for choosing a language that is close to your heart and is already a part of your life is that it can make your child's path to bilingualism easier and more straightforward.

2. I moved to the country where I'm living as an adult, and I'm not fluent in the language that's predominantly spoken here. It's easier for me for me to speak to my child in my native language. Will I be putting my child at a disadvantage by not speaking in the language that most people around us speak?

Parents who are not fluent in the language that is predominantly spoken in their country of residence often worry that their children will have a harder time in school if they do not speak with them in that language. They fear that because they have difficulty with speaking the country's language, their children will too. But there is no evidence to support this. On the contrary, there is no reason to believe that a child will not pick up the predominantly spoken language in school, if taught properly. (In Steps 6 and 7, I discuss reading and writing in a second language and bilingualism and school in greater depth.)

Linguists agree that parents who struggle to speak the language of the country where they're living, but who speak another language fluently, should be encouraged to speak with their child in the language they know best. In their native language, these parents will use an array of expressions, comparisons, and idioms, all with the correct flow, accent, and intonation. When speaking their native language, parents are also much more likely to sing nursery rhymes, recite poems, and tell stories to their child.

This is important because it leads to a much more varied and elaborate language "input" for the child, and the quality of language that a child is exposed to goes a long way in determining how well he learns the language. In addition, higher level language skills do more than help us speak, read, and write in a particular language with ease: They are crucial for developing a higher level thought process, regardless of what language is spoken.

3. I (or my partner) can speak a second language a little bit, but far from perfectly. Should we still choose to teach that language to our child?

There are many parents who may be not fluent in a second language, but who can speak it a little bit. Speaking to your baby in that language, even if it is somewhat broken, can be a great way to start your child on the path toward bilingualism.

Also, interestingly enough, you don't have to speak a language well, much less fluently, to teach language skills to your children! "When my wife and I got married, she spoke a little German, but I couldn't speak it myself," Brian says. "Still, we decided that when we had kids, she would speak to them in German, with the goal that they would become bilingual. When our two daughters were young, I would read bedtime stories to them in German even though I did not understand a word of what I was reading. I could do this because German is quite a phonetic language. The kids understood though, and it still amazes me that they went along with this. Now I am studying German, and I can finally understand those stories!"

As your child grows older, you probably will have to look farther afield to provide him with the necessary instruction and practice he'll need to keep progressing. (I discuss ways to increase second language exposure in depth in Step 4.) But if you learn the second language along with your child, it will make the experience more natural and family oriented, and you may not have to look quite as far!

4. We're going to be living in a foreign country. If we choose to learn the language, won't we just pick it up while we're there?

Some families find themselves moving to a foreign country for job reasons. While you might pick up some of the language just by living there, in most countries—including some of the poorest countries in the world—it's possible to get by just speaking English. School, too, may be taught in English. (This will definitely be the case if your child attends an American or International school.) That's why I encourage parents in this situation to develop bilingual goals and a plan for achieving them just as they would if they were living at home.

I can't tell you how many families I've met who have returned home, sometimes years later, without learning the language of the country where they were living. "We thought we were only going to be there for a couple of years," they tell me. "Then two years became three, four. . . . Yet we never got down to thinking seriously about learning the language, so it never happened."

So, if your family is planning to live abroad, I recommend asking yourself: Would I like our family to learn the local language? If the answer is yes, then use Step 4 to create a Bilingual Action Plan. I also advise starting to learn the language as soon as possible, even before you move.

Remember, too, that when it comes to languages, it's either "use it or lose it." The brain is programmed to adapt to its environment and will not store information that is no longer used or needed, including a language.

So when you return home, you'll need to create a *new* Action Plan, this one for maintaining the language. When her family returned home to the United States after living in Italy for seven years, Marcy, for example, took it upon herself to help her sons keep up their Italian.

"It felt a little strange to be back home in the U.S. and speaking Italian," she says. "But I knew that I was doing the right thing, because within weeks the boys, who had spoken only Italian to each other when we were in Italy, were speaking to each other in English. Even though my Italian wasn't perfect, I believe it kept them from losing the language completely. Perhaps the proof is in the pudding. They each spent one of their college years in Rome!"

5. But am I limiting my child by choosing just two languages?

Keep in mind that the languages that you choose now will be the ones that you orchestrate mostly from home. There's no reason that your child can't take advantage of opportunities to learn a third language (or even more) in the future.

Some parents are concerned that if their child is already bilingual, adding on a third language might be too much for the child's brain and could lead to confusion. But there is no evidence that shows that children, or adults, for that matter, cannot learn multiple languages. In fact, research shows that when a bilingual child attempts to learn a third language, he will actually progress faster and more easily than his monolingual peers who are learning their second language. This makes sense, as the bilingual child's "linguistic brain machinery" is more developed. You do, however, want to make sure that your child has enough exposure in each language to develop solid skills in that language. It's not that your child's brain is incapable of learning three languages simultaneously; it's just that his brain will require a lot of language input in all three languages to do so, which can be a real challenge to pull off. (Although the focus of this book is on bilingualism, I will address the process of learning multiple languages and offer tips for how go about it as we proceed through the Steps.)

6. But how do I choose if my spouse and I both speak more than one language?

On the one hand, a child's brain is naturally wired to learn several languages, but if you want to increase the chances for your child to consolidate her proficiency in multiple languages it is important to try to go about it in an orderly manner. Here's why: If there are no guidelines as to who speaks which language when (I address how to establish these guidelines in the next two Steps), a child might learn, for example, some Spanish from listening to his parents speak to each other in Spanish, some Portuguese from overhearing his grandparents who babysit him speak to each other in that language, and a little English because his well-intentioned parents and grandparents speak to him in broken English. But under these circumstances, sadly, the child doesn't become truly proficient in *any* of the languages and won't until he enters kindergarten and learns English at school.

Another situation that can arise in multilingual families is that the language (or languages) that are spoken to a child can shift over the years. The family might move to another country or move closer to relatives who speak a different language, or the family members who help care for the children can change. If your family is multilingual, advance planning will help you avoid exposing your child to a new language until he has established a solid foundation in the main languages you have chosen for him.

To help narrow your language choices down, revisit the Language Questionnaire (Worksheet 1) that you filled out on page 29. Also, ask yourself:

- Which language do I feel connected to?
- Which language am I most proficient in?
- Which language can I most easily find support for (such as extended family members who can speak to your child in that language)?

But as difficult as the decision may be, try not to become paralyzed by it. Remember, that putting off bilingualism can mean never starting bilingualism.

7 Things to Remember
When Choosing a Second Language for Your Child

1. Choosing *a language that you love and that feels natural* can make your child's path toward bilingualism easier and more straightforward.
2. *Monolingual parents can transfer important language skills to their children* even if they do not speak a second language perfectly.
3. *Adults are very capable of learning other languages,* and can do so along with their children.
4. *If you're not fluent in English,* it's not only acceptable to *speak to your child in your native language,* linguists encourage it. In addition to helping your child become fluent in that language, you'll help him develop higher language skills, which can help him learn English more easily later on.
5. *Multilingual families do need to decide on which languages* they wish their child to learn and plan to maintain language consistency and ensure a "consolidation" of skills.
6. Choosing a second language that you are going to orchestrate from home *does not mean that your child cannot learn a third language* later on, for example, at school.
7. *Take into account the resources that are available* to you that can support your bilingual goals long term.

Q&A: *My son's school has a second language program at school. Every three years the second language curriculum moves on to another language. He just started studying Mandarin-Chinese and three years from now it will be French. I am concerned that with this frequent switching of languages he won't become proficient in any second language.*

As the cognitive and cultural advantages of bilingualism have started to be recognized, there has been a boom of "multicultural" and "multilingual" activities in schools, from language "exposure" programs such as the one described to teaching preschoolers to count to ten in half a dozen languages. Understanding the different cultures is often the main goal of these programs, and it is an important and worthy one. But, unfortunately, these short-term programs do not promote the type of long-term learning that is ultimately necessary to achieve bilingualism.

4. Set a Start Date

There are two major ways that a child can become bilingual. The first is when a child is exposed simultaneously during his first three years or so to two languages. This is called **simultaneous bilingualism.** The second is when a child learns one language first, and then later, learns a second language. This is called **sequential bilingualism.**

How does simultaneous bilingualism work?

When a child learns two languages simultaneously from a very early age, his brain does the same job for both languages, and the process is essentially the same as it is for a child who is only learning one language. First, the child says single words in each language, then puts two words together in each language, and then builds more and more complex sentences. But here's where a bilingual and a monolingual child are different: Bilingual children will mix languages. In other words, when they're speaking a sentence in one language, they might use a word or two from the other. This is entirely to be expected as the child's brain is still developing and has not yet fully mastered how to separate the languages. It is only a question of time before it does. As the child's brain develops, and as he learns more words, he will become more successful at separating the vocabulary of both languages. (I address mixing of languages in greater depth in Step 5.)

Many people think that children who learn two languages simultaneously start speaking later than children who learn just one, but, in fact, both monolingual and bilingual children say their first words at around 8 to 15 months. As I mentioned in Step 1, if your child does start to speak later, but is able to *understand* well, then most likely, the delay is only a minor one. Again, if you're concerned about your child's language development, I do encourage you to have her assessed by a speech and language pathologist. (I will speak in more detail about bilingual children and language delay in Step 7.)

How does sequential bilingualism work?

Many children learn one language during their first years, and learn another later on. For example, some children speak a language other than English at home, and then learn English when they enter preschool or kindergarten.

Typically when a young child who is already proficient in one language is thrown into a new environment where he must learn a second to communicate, he'll start with phrases that are vital to expressing his wants and needs, such as "give me," "what next," "can I play?" In this way the child is no different than the adult tourist in a foreign country who makes it a priority to learn key phrases, such as "where is the bathroom?" Both the tourist and the child are simply doing what they need to do to survive in a new environment.

A solid first language can actually be helpful when it comes to learning a second language, because skills from the first language can be transferred to the second. For instance, a child who already has one language under his belt will try to speak in more complex sentences in the second language, too. In addition, from a brain perspective, the child will use the skills that he has already developed in his first language as a starting point for learning the second. And, at first, the child will mix the two languages because he is using the stronger language to support the developing one. As skills in the second language progress, the amount of "mixing" between the first and second languages gradually decreases. Usually, after around one to two years of speaking the second language, children can talk with their friends and express their thoughts with ease.

41

More challenging, however, is when middle school or high school students are suddenly dropped into a school where classes are taught in a language other than the one they speak. These students are usually able to carry on a conversation in the new language after one or two years, but these skills are short of what's needed to do the more academic class work that requires higher level language skills. (I'll visit this situation in greater depth in Step 7.)

When it comes to adding another language, there is no hard and fast rule as to exactly when it should (or should not) be done. What is more important than the timing is ensuring that you continue to consolidate your child's skills in her first language while introducing the second. That means continuing to provide your child with solid input in her first language. Doing this ensures that your child will:

- continue to develop more complex language skills in her first language, while learning skills in the second language.
- use the solid language skills from the first language to accelerate learning in the second language.

Which is better: simultaneous or sequential bilingualism?

Children can learn two languages well simultaneously or seqentially, as long as they get sufficient instruction and practice in both languages. But I believe that simultaneous bilingualism from birth is easier, which is why I urge parents to start speaking to their baby in two languages, literally, from day one. And by "easier" I mean mainly easier for you, the parent. Because while a child's brain can adapt to learning another language down the line, it can be quite challenging for a parent to suddenly switch to talking with her child in a language that's different from the one they've spoken together for four, five (or more) years. Plus, if you start at birth there's more time—and less pressure—before school enters the picture. And finally, I really can't stress enough, postponing bilingualism can mean never starting bilingualism.

**If You Do Opt for Sequential Bilingualism,
These 7 Tips Can Make It Easier:**

1. *Start little by little.* Be aware that your child might resist an abrupt change of language.
2. Initially, you might be supporting understanding by *translating,* but the goal is to *stop doing this little by little.*
3. *Start speaking the language during chosen times or activities when you're not rushed* and there is plenty of extra time for explanations. For example, Sunday morning breakfasts might be a time when you feel relaxed. You don't want to put yourself in the situation of being stressed to get kids out of the door and teaching vocabulary. Then add on one activity at a time. For instance, add on bath time and teach the vocabulary words related to bath time.
4. Switch to *reading simple books* in the second language, simplifying and translating if needed. Books are a great way to teach new words.
5. *Gradually extend the amount of time* you speak the language and add on resources and activities that your kids can do on the computer or TV, for example.
6. *Encourage your child to respond* to you in the second language.
7. Don't give up! Remember, *time is on your side.*

Q&A: *Our daughter is very shy and does not speak much in her French-speaking preschool, even though French is her first (and, so far, only) language. Soon she'll be going to an English-speaking kindergarten. Should we be concerned that she is going to shut down and not talk there at all?*

Sometimes children who are shy withdraw when faced with a new language in a new environment. And if they feel extremely anxious about it, they might even go through what is called a "silent period." When this occurs, the child does not talk at all in the new environment, much less in the new language. But it is important to understand that the underlying difficulty is the anxiety and new environment more than the new language. As a child becomes more comfortable, makes friends, and starts to learn the language, she will speak more. Parents can also take steps to help ease the transition to the new school—and help alleviate their child's anxiety about it. Visit the school before classes start. Meet the teacher. Play on the school playground. And over the summer, try to meet at least one child who will be in the same class. But if a child continues not to speak in school after sufficient amount of adjustment time, parents should consult their pediatrician. It might be a sign of a larger anxiety disorder, and your doctor can recommend a professional who can help.

5. Determine How Proficient You Hope Your Child Will Be in a Second Language

Do you want your children to be able to simply understand their visiting grandparents from Japan? To be capable of taking an active part in the conversation? Do you think it's important for your children to be able to read and write as well as speak a second language?

Determining the proficiency level you want your children to achieve in each language is very important because it will directly affect the decisions that you make and the actions that you take.

For example, when Maria, a single parent and native Spanish speaker, increased her work hours, she was torn between placing her daughter Inez in an English-speaking daycare center near her work, sending her to a morning English-speaking preschool, or putting her in a family daycare run by her cousin that was closer to home. Because it is very important for Maria that her daughter be equally fluent in both English and Spanish, she developed a plan that was a little more complicated for her to pull off, but gave her daughter exposure to both languages. She opted to put Inez in the English-language preschool three mornings a week, but had her Spanish-speaking cousin take her every afternoon, essentially immersing Inez in English in the mornings and Spanish in the afternoons.

Linguists describe levels of bilingual proficiency in many different ways. But here is a quick guide:

Level 1: Being able to understand a second language. This level is sometimes called "passive" bilingualism because while the person understands the language, she doesn't "actively" speak.

Level 2: Being able to speak a second language, more or less fluently. At this level a person can carry on a conversation in the language and express her thoughts with ease.

Level 3: Being able to speak, read, and write in two languages. It's important to note, though, that even people who can speak, read, and write fluently in two languages usually have a stronger or more dominant language. It is unusual to be a so-called "balanced bilingual," which is someone who is equally highly proficient in both languages.

One level is not necessarily better than another, but as proficiency increases it is thought that the positive effect on the brain brought about by bilingualism increases, too. And once a person attains one level, he is well positioned to reach the next. For example, a child who grows up understanding a second language will most likely learn to speak it more quickly and easily than a person who is starting from scratch.

Q&A: *I speak Japanese with my husband and English with my children. Will my children pick up any Japanese at all, just by hearing us talk?*

This scenario (parents speaking to each other in one language but in English, or in another language, to their child) or a similar one (such as a child spending time with extended family members who speak another language) is quite common in bilingual or multilingual families. I once discussed this very question with a bilingual speech and language therapist, and she put it very simply: "A child does not go around with his hands on his ears. When he is hearing the other language, he is in fact listening to it, trying to make sense of it. And if the child hears that language frequently, he will at the very least develop some understanding of it." So children in this situation usually will develop "passive bilingualism," and very often speak some simple sentences in the language as well. Additionally, they will usually identify with the second language and culture in a positive way.

6. Do a Reality Check. Are Your Proficiency Goals Realistic for Your Family?

Keep in mind that as language proficiency goals increase, so will:

1. the amount of language input required.
2. the complexity of language input required. (For example, if you want your child to be able to read and write as well as speak the language, you'll need written materials.)
3. the amount of time required to achieve the goal.

One of the most frequent difficulties that I see parents run into is setting the bar at the highest level (balanced bilingualism), but not planning for the time and extensive amount of language exposure that is needed to achieve it. Keep in mind that the level of proficiency your child achieves is going to be directly tied to the amount of time he spends speaking and studying the language. Therefore, **it is very important to match your bilingual goal with the amount of time and effort you and your child can devote to the second language.** Otherwise, it's easy to get discouraged and give up on the second language all together.

Often parents expect that a second language can be fully learned in a year or two. As I've mentioned, a child who frequently hears and

46

speaks a second language often can speak it well enough to carry on a conversation after that amount of time. But it's important to know that if you want your child to develop higher level academic skills in the second language, such as reading and writing, it usually extends the time frame to five or ten years. But the great thing about goals is that they can always be reevaluated! I encourage parents to reevaluate the level of language proficiency they're aiming for with some degree of regularity so that it stays in sync with the amount of language input your child is getting.

Keep in mind, too, that even as a child is progressing toward proficiency in two languages, his experiences in both languages will be different. Because experience fuels learning, a child is going to develop different skills and strengths in each language. For instance, your child might use one language in school, and the other language at home and with friends and family members.

7. Take into Account That One Language Will Be Dominant

When parents set out to raise their child bilingual, they sometimes believe that the child will speak both languages with exactly the same degree of fluency. But the truth is in the reality of everyday life, bilingual people usually use one language more than the other and that language becomes the stronger, or dominant, language. So, it's important to remind yourself that while your child might speak and even read and write fluently in two languages, most likely one will be his dominant language.

But dominance can shift easily, thanks to brain "plasticity." The brain is made this way because it is engineered toward survival. So if your child goes to a school or moves to a country where his less dominant language is the one that's primarily spoken, it's likely that that language will soon become his dominant one.

That's what happened to Joseph. He took German in high school and college, and once he started working as an accountant, he continued to study German through courses that he did from home. When he went for his MBA, he enrolled in a German university, and when he got his degree, he got a job in Berlin. "I think I knew that learning German would inevitably expand my horizons and lead me to new opportunities and experiences," he says. "But I don't think I ever quite imagined that it would lead to my living and working in Germany one day, and that I would feel more comfortable speaking German than I do English!"

A second language does take years to learn. But try not to be daunted by that fact. *Remember that time is on your side.* You and your child have years ahead of you. And literally, it's one word after another. All you have to do is start with one word, and then build on it. *Right now, starting is the most important thing to do.* I promise you will feel encouraged by each sign of progress that your child makes!

To help you formulate your bilingual goals, fill out Worksheet 2 on the next page. Again, it can be helpful for both parents to fill it out, either together or at separate times (and then compare responses).

Step 2 Wrap-Up: My Bilingual Goals and Choices

The most important reasons why I want to raise a child bilingual are:

If you and/or your partner is bilingual:

The language that I choose to speak to my child is:

The language that my partner chooses to speak to our child is:

The language that our child's caregiver(s) and/or relatives will speak to our child is:

If both you and your partner are monolingual:

The language that I choose to speak to our child is:

The language that my partner chooses to speak to our child is:

The language that our child's caregiver(s) and/or relatives will speak to our child is:

We are going to start to speak to our child in those languages:

at birth

other date: ___ / ___ / ___

The level of bilingualism I want my child to achieve is:

On a level from 1 to 10, with 1 being "unimportant" and 10 being "extremely important", my level of commitment to my child's bilingualism is: _____

3

Becoming a
Bilingual Coach

Now that you understand how bilingualism works and you've defined your bilingual goals, you may be thinking, "I know I want to do this, but *how* do I do it?" or "Where on Earth do I begin?" In this Step, which is divided into two parts, I will walk you through the process of becoming what I call a bilingual coach.

Part One: Taking Charge helps you become comfortable with the role of bilingual coach.
Part Two: Who Speaks Which Language When? helps you decide what your family's ground rules will be.

Part One: Taking Charge

To achieve your bilingual goals for your child, you'll need to take on the role of planner and coach. That may sound overwhelming, but it's actually a role that you, as a parent, already play every day. You and your partner undoubtedly spend much of your time thinking about and coming up with ways to meet your child's needs and help him achieve his short- and long-term goals, whether it's getting to soccer practice this afternoon or getting into college several years from now. And when you think about it, much of parenting involves coaching, from toilet training your toddler to teaching your teen to drive. It's just that when it comes to bilingualism, your role as coach is omnipresent instead of being limited to just one specific activity.

Your major tasks as bilingual planner and coach will be:

1. making your child's bilingualism a priority for yourself and your child—and conveying its importance to your child.
2. ensuring your child gets the proper amount of language input to match the proficiency level you hope to reach.
3. giving, or arranging for, language instruction.

1. Making bilingualism a priority for you and your child

Mary-Margaret, who is monolingual, wants her daughter Susan, a first grader, to become bilingual in French and English. The elementary school that Susan attends offers after-school French classes, so Mary-Margaret signed Susan up and considered the classes to be a cornerstone of her Bilingual Action Plan. But after a few weeks, Mary-Margaret felt guilty because Susan was missing out on playdates as a result of the French classes. "Susan was upset that all her friends were having playdates without her," Mary-Margaret told me. In the end, she let Susan skip multiple French classes to be with her friends.

A mother myself, I know firsthand that as parents we feel our children's pain often almost as acutely as our children. But by giving in, Mary-Margaret created a problem in that she sent conflicting messages to Susan: Her mother says she wants her to learn French, but then she allows her to skip French classes so as not to miss out on playdates. Any child would be left wondering, is learning a second language important or not?

If you express ambivalence about your decision to teach your child a second language, your child will pick up on that ambivalence right away. And in most cases, he'll be less likely to want to put forth the effort that it takes to achieve bilingualism. As in so many parenting situations, consistency is key when it comes to raising your child to be bilingual.

Bilingual parents who feel torn between their attachment to their heritage and their assimilation into mainstream American culture may also struggle with making the hard choices that are sometimes necessary to ensure their child gets enough language input to become bilingual. But if you express pride in your heritage, your child will understand *why* you want him to learn your language—and why it's worth the effort on both your parts.

In all the interviews that I have done over the years with children, it continues to surprise and sadden me how often children try to keep their bilingualism a secret, and how unaware they are of the great treasure that they hold. I remember telling Joo-Eun, a second grader, "Wow, you can speak Korean. That's amazing! I cannot speak a word of Korean. I would love it if you would say a sentence in Korean." Joo-Eun's response? "I'm too embarrassed," she said.

You want your child to grow up feeling proud of who he is and where he came from and proud of his ability to speak more than one language. I've found that one of the best ways to transmit this sense of ownership and pride is to simply have ongoing, open-ended discussions with your child about why it is important to you that he learn your language, or a second language, and how special it is to be able to speak more than one language. It's not that you are asking him whether he wants to learn the language, but rather that you are explaining (in an age-appropriate way) where you are coming from and expressing how much you want your language and your world to become his language and his world, too. When kids assert things like, "he's not my daddy; he's my *papa*," it's a reflection not only of how seriously they take language (drawing the distinction between "daddy" and "papa"), but also of the special bond that a shared language creates between parents and children. In my experience, when parents express their bilingual goals as a desire to share, it usually results in a greater willingness on the part of their child to embrace those goals and view the effort as a joint endeavor.

2. Ensuring the correct amount of language input

In most educational situations involving your child (school, of course, being the prime example), the decisions about what your child learns and when are left to others. As a parent, you typically play a supporting role, through supervising homework, for example. But when you're the one orchestrating your child's learning of a language—and in many cases, doing the actual teaching of it yourself—those decisions are made by you.

Obviously, you do not have to go out and buy books and materials, say, for the next ten years. But as I mentioned at the beginning of Step 2, bilingualism—indeed the mastery of any language—really comes down to one word building on another. So, it's imperative to come up with concrete ways (and a schedule!) to ensure that your child gets the proper amount of language input today, this week, and this month to achieve the level of bilingualism you're aiming for years down the road. Later, I offer lots of ideas for how to maximize language input. As you read, consider how you might implement each idea (or how you might modify it to work better for your family) and when you might start incorporating it into your weekly schedule.

3. Teaching, or arranging for, language instruction

For many parents, being the bilingual coach often means you're the teacher of the foreign language as well. And it can be difficult to be a parent/coach/teacher simultaneously. (As Tom Baker, Steve Martin's character in the movie *Cheaper by the Dozen*, put it, "Right now, I am not a father, I am a coach.") And as any parent, bilingual or otherwise, who has gone to battle over homework knows, there are times when "being nice" simply doesn't get the job done!

Further on, I will explain how you can teach your child a second language, but the most important thing to remember is that language learning does not have to entail dreary grammar drills and

Troubleshooting Guide: 7 Frequent Situations and Where to Find the Solutions in this Book.

Frequent situations	Where you can find a solution
You feel inadequate in speaking the language.	Step 2; Step 5
Your child senses ambivalence on your part about her bilingualism and resists the language.	Step 3; Step 5
Your child does not identify with the language in a positive manner and/or with a sense of pride.	Step 2; Step 3; Step 5
You're finding it challenging to make language input interesting and fun.	Step 4; Resource List
You're feeling discouraged because your child is taking more time than you expected to learn the language.	Step 7
Your child seems to be resisting the language or having more trouble learning it than his siblings.	Step 5; Step 7
You're finding it difficult to modify your Bilingual Action Plan as you go along.	Step 5; Step 7

flash cards! It can and should be incorporated into fun family activities. You want your child to feel motivated to learn the language because it's important to you, but you also need to feed that motivation by making the process enjoyable, interesting, and relevant to your child's life. Research shows that this is the best way to ensure that children learn and remember what they're being taught, regardless of whether it's a language, a math or science concept, or a reading or writing skill.

Pierre took this advice to heart one delightful spring afternoon when he and his kids went digging under rocks, Pierre's kids didn't just learn about the natural world; they also learned French. As Pierre held up various objects—rocks, twigs, leaves, bugs, worms—he would name them in French. In the course of the afternoon, he also told his children about the hard work his grandfather did as a potato farmer in his native Canada and how he helped out his grandfather on the family farm every summer.

In a single afternoon, Pierre's children—who live in the United States and mostly speak English—absorbed lessons about nature and learned a smattering of new French words and about their family heritage, all while having fun digging in the dirt. And, you can bet that the afternoon and everything learned during it will be etched in the minds of Pierre's children for a long time to come.

Part Two: Who Speaks Which Language When?

There are many strategies for teaching your child your language, but I'll begin with what is arguably the most effective and the most straightforward to execute: **One-Parent-One-Language, or OPOL.** As the name suggests, one parent speaks one language to the child, and the other parent speaks another—*always.*

Maria and her husband Mario have used the OPOL method with their son Emmanuel since he was born. Maria speaks to Emmanuel, now 3, in Spanish, and Mario speaks to him in Portuguese. He goes to an English-speaking daycare. Maria and Mario usually speak Spanish together, but Mario mixes in a lot of Portuguese words. Even so, since Emmanuel began to talk, he has only spoken Spanish to his mother and Portuguese to his father. As expected, he still mixes Spanish and Portuguese a little. Yet his daycare providers report that he never speaks any Spanish or Portuguese words to them. This is typical of a child brought up using the OPOL method. As young as he is, Emmanuel is already aware that the daycare providers do not understand his other languages.

In short, the key to OPOL's success is that it allows parents to effectively surmount *all* of the major hurdles to bilingualism, from lack of consistency to a lack of language input. However, I rate "supports consistency" as the number one advantage to OPOL for a reason.

---

6 Reasons Why One-Parent-One-Language Is Such a Successful Way to Raise a Bilingual Child.

1. It *supports consistency.*
2. It is *simple* for parents to carry out.
3. It's *effortless to set up a language boundary* (an understanding of which family members and/or other caregivers speak which language, and when). As with Emmanuel, if one parent *always* speaks one language and the other parent another, even very young children can easily understand and respect the language boundary.
4. It *naturally leads to the child responding* to the parent in the same language.
5. It enables *two or more languages* to be spoken to the child in an orderly way.
6. It enables a child to receive a *maximum language input* in two different languages, because the parent and child use the language to communicate no matter what the circumstance, time of the day, or activity.

I've found that once parents jump into their Bilingual Action Plan, perhaps *the* greatest hurdle is maintaining consistency. One-Parent-One-Language is the easiest way to provide consistent language input. With OPOL, you don't have to carve out time to sit down and formally instruct your child—or remember whether it's French-speaking-Sunday-morning-brunch or homework-in-Armenian-Tuesday. Your child simply learns the language by being spoken to and speaking it back—the same way that a monolingual child learns a language from his parent. In many circumstances, the primary factor that separates a person who speaks fluently from a person who merely understands a second language is the amount of language input. Generally, OPOL generates more language input than any other method.

Q&A: *My husband works long hours and therefore has limited time to speak with our daughter in Ukrainian. Will she still learn the language?*

Perhaps not surprisingly, research shows that there is a direct correlation between language input and the speed of language acquisition. So a child who receives limited language input can be expected to learn that language at a slower pace than a child who receives more. Even with limited exposure, though, the little girl referred to in this question will probably learn to understand everyday, commonly used sentences in Ukrainian relatively quickly. However, it will probably take her longer to master more complex vocabulary and to actually learn to speak Ukrainian than it would if her father were able to speak with her more.

Remember from Step 2 that it is important to match your bilingual goals with the amount of time you and your child can devote to the language. If the two are not in sync it's easy to feel that your child is failing to progress, and give up altogether. So, as I would advise the mother who posed this question, keep your expectations realistic over the years, be patient for results, and consider seeking out other ways to increase language input. (For ideas, see Step 4 and the Resource List at the end of the book.)

OPOL effortlessly and very effectively creates a clearly identifiable language boundary. Rachel and her husband are raising their daughter, Christine, 7, to be bilingual in French and English. "Christine speaks only French to her dad," Rachel told me. "I can speak some French, but I speak only English to Christine. If I ever try to speak to her in French, she is absolutely adamant that this is *not* okay. Even if I speak to her in French to spare her the embarrassment of being told off in front of her friends, she gets very upset, and starts yelling as if to drown my voice, 'that's not your language, you're not allowed to use it.'"

I often hear toddlers and preschoolers talk about "Mommy's language" or "Daddy's language." As one father told me, "When we took Katherine to Greece for the first time she was amazed that 'they all speak Daddy's language!'"

When Stefano returned home each afternoon from his English-speaking preschool, he would tell his parents about everything he had done there. He identified so strongly with speaking Spanish to them that he translated everything, even the songs. To this day, his parents love to sing Stefano's Spanish version of "London Bridge Is Falling Down"!

Finally, OPOL can help multilingual families avoid language chaos. As I discussed in Step 2, multilingual homes are by their very nature complex linguistic environments. Parents might speak together in English, but speak with their extended families in other languages. One parent might not even be able to understand, much less be fluent in, all the languages that the other parent speaks. In such cases, it can be a significant challenge to create an environment where a child can master, in an orderly fashion, two or more languages with solid proficiency. OPOL allows each parent to speak a different language to the child, regardless of whether the other parent understands the other language or not. Furthermore, to keep things orderly, and boost language input, each of the parent's extended family members can speak to the child in the same language the parent does. If English is not one of the languages the parents choose to speak to their child, the child can then add it on as a language he learns outside the home, at school and from interacting with his friends and the community.

But as successful as One-Parent-One-Language is for raising children bilingually, there is one predictable obstacle that parents who choose it often encounter: hesitation to speak to their child in public in that language. I'll offer tips for overcoming this self-consciousness in Step 5.

Another Option: Variations on OPOL

There are multiple variations of One-Parent-One-Language that can also be very successful. But for these variations to work, they must adhere to the same basic premise as OPOL: a clearly identifiable person (or group of people) who *always* speak to the child in the same language. Like OPOL, such scenarios can provide both consistency and clear language boundaries—two necessary ingredients for achieving proficiency in two languages.

For example, oftentimes both parents work and children end up spending a great deal of time with extended family members or other caregivers. If grandparents, aunts, uncles, and/or babysitters speak to the child in the same language that the parents do, it ensures the child will basically get the same amount of language input that he would if he were with the parent full time. Alternatively, certain extended family members or a caregiver may be the ones designated to speak to the child in the chosen second language. Remember the Chinese babysitter whom Jennifer hired. She was the one to speak and later teach Jennifer's daughters, Mandarin.

The fact that these variations can work quite well for raising a bilingual child is a reminder that none of us, including young children, live in a cocoon of the immediate family unit. Even before children attend kindergarten, where they're usually immersed in English, they often attend daycare or preschool and participate in at least one organized activity, all of which often exposes them to English. So, to reiterate what I said in Step 2, a family that decides to speak a language, or languages, other than English at home should not be concerned their child will not master English, especially once he reaches school age.

A Third Way: Using Language Boundaries

If One-Parent-One-Language or a variation is not feasible for your family, another way is to speak the language in specific, predetermined situations, such as at mealtimes or on weekends. To put it another way, you draw the language boundaries around situations rather than people. But because in this case the language input is

---

3 Examples of Language Boundaries:

Boundaries depending on *time of day*
- Mealtimes
- On weekends

Boundaries depending on *location*
- One language within the home; another language outside of the home
- The whole family speaks another language at the grandparents' home

Boundaries depending on an *activity*
- When doing homework, for instance speaking French during French homework
- When playing soccer on a predominantly Spanish-speaking team
- When the tutor comes once a week
- When watching TV or using the Internet. For example, you can tell your child he must watch the broadcast of the baseball game in Spanish or switch the search engine to another language when looking up something online.

---

typically much less, it's essential that you and your child are clear on, and most importantly, keep to the boundaries you set up. This is often easier said than done, so this method tends to work best when both parents and children are enthusiastic about the second language. If your child enjoys learning the language, he's more likely to be motivated to make the most of the speaking time he does have.

But do keep in mind that in the reality of everyday life, with kids especially, one activity often blends into another, and despite your best intentions, your carefully set up language boundaries can become blurred. For example, if you and your kids are eating dinner moments before you head out door for one child's judo practice (while simultaneously checking that your child has all of his judo gear and his brother has all his homework in his backpack to do while waiting for the practice to be over), do you redirect your children repeatedly to speak to you in Japanese because it's mealtime? In real life, it is difficult to repeatedly redirect a child to speak a certain language, unless the child specifically wants to. So with this method, the motivation of the child and positive self-identification with the language play a crucial role in its success.

Many parents ask me, "Can my child really learn a second language with the language boundary method?" and "Is it worth the effort?" Although it's true that with this method a child's primary language usually remains strongly dominant, and it will probably be more challenging for him to achieve a high level proficiency in the second language, the answer is still an emphatic "yes."

Many parents, including Amira, who speaks fluent Arabic (and could have chosen the OPOL route), decide the language boundary method is the way for their families to go. When Amira's son Kamir was a toddler she became interested in raising him bilingual. "But from the start," she says, "I envisioned it as a fun, side activity for both of us, rather than a full-time commitment." She started by speaking with Kamir in Arabic during bath time, and as the years have gone by, she has simply added some activities and moved on to others. "We did bedtime stories in Arabic for a time," she says, "when I got my hands on a great kids' version of *The Arabian Nights* with wonderful illustrations. We've also done getting dressed in Arabic, cooking, and 'good night.' In fact, 'good night' is still part of the bedtime ritual now."

Kamir, now 11, understands quite a bit of Arabic. He often stays with his maternal grandmother who speaks Arabic and barely any English, and they're able to communicate just fine. "It's been, and continues to be, a great experience, and in all truth, a lot of fun" Amira says. "Equally important, it has not felt daunting or stressful at all." For Amira, using the language boundary method kept her and her son enthusiastic about learning Arabic.

Although linguists do not all agree on the outcome for children with a mixed array of language input, a child with normal language ability will probably pick up some language with any strategy that the parent chooses. Remember, your child's brain is a formidable machine that is built to make sense of languages coming in and to learn them. So, do not shy away from whatever strategy you think will work for you.

And what I often see happen is that even with relatively little language input, most children pick up some understanding of the language, and in some cases, even develop a remarkable degree of proficiency. Then parents, surprised and pleased at their child's progress and interest, reevaluate their bilingual goals and "upgrade" their Bilingual Action Plan, which I will guide you through creating in the next chapter. For example, when Amira and Kamir were recently deciding on his first sleep-away camp, he suggested a foreign-language one! The ability—and flexibility—to adapt your Bilingual Action Plan as you go along is a key part of successfully raising a bilingual child. I'll offer tips for how to adapt your Plan to changing circumstances in Step 7.

Creating Your Bilingual Action Plan

Your Bilingual Action Plan is a roadmap for turning your bilingual goals for your child into reality. While it's true that families who live in urban areas, with their multiethnic neighborhoods and easier access to bilingual resources, might seem to have greater opportunities for outside support, don't get discouraged if it seems as though your area is homogenous and monolingual. This Step is designed to inform you and excite you about the bilingual enrichment opportunities that are available to you no matter where you live. I also encourage you to refer to the Resource List at the end of the book. It provides an "at-a-glance" guide to the resources mentioned in this Step and throughout the book.

This Step is broken down into five parts. By the end of the Step you will be able to identify the key components of your Bilingual Action Plan and create a weekly bilingual schedule for your family.

Part One: Maximizing Language Input at Home
Part Two: Making the Most of Community and Family Resources
Part Three: Finding School Support
Part Four: How Three Families Are Raising Bilingual Children
Part Five: Create Your Own Bilingual Action Plan

Part One: Maximizing Language Input at Home

The good news is that whatever method you choose for teaching your child your language, there is an array of resources that can provide additional language input—and give you a chance to rest your vocal chords!

Rosemarie, who is raising her two daughters, Simone and Vivianne, to be bilingual in French and English, says, "I feel like I'm constantly working to eliminate all English other than homework from our home, because I want French to be spoken there as much as possible. The first thing I do when I pick up a DVD is to turn it over and check the languages to make sure there's a French version. I admit that trying to turn every activity into a French-speaking one is a never-ending challenge, but when I see how far the girls have come with their French and how they continue to improve, it's makes it all worthwhile."

The farther you can extend the language boundary at home, the more your kids will benefit. But you should not feel overwhelmed by the effort, either. You need to create language boundaries that will work for you and your family. For example, you might say to your child that he can watch television "if you watch it in Spanish" or look up something on the Internet "if it is on Wikipedia in German."

When planning activities at home, keep in mind what research has shown about how babies and children learn best. To put it very simply, babies are wired to learn about their environments to survive. So they are attentive to language input in any language. Kids learn better and retain more of what they learn when they're interested and engaged. So when it comes to kids and language input, the attractiveness of the activities is every bit as important as the sheer number of them.

Technology

What's the easiest way to create language input activities that will be attractive to your child? Use technology! Technology increases language input and can get a child excited about language learning.

Parents often ask me if *anything* done in front of a screen can really teach children. You're wise to be skeptical, and let me state emphatically that I am *not* suggesting that you park your child in front of the computer or TV set for hours in the name of increasing his language input!

The American Academy of Pediatrics (AAP) guidelines recommend that children (preschoolers to adolescents) spend no more than one to two hours per day watching "quality TV and/or videos," and that children under two years of age watch no television at all. However, most education specialists recognize the huge potential of technology when it comes to learning and point out that the computer, for example, is fast becoming an indispensable educational

---

Why Technology Is a Strong Second Language Partner

- It can make language acquisition activities more palatable, leading to *increased time* spent listening to and learning the language.
- It can make learning *interactive,* which means that your child gets to actively participate and answer questions rather than passively absorbing information.
- It allows you, the parent, to *tailor activities* to your child's age, ability level, and interests, which is important to maximize learning.
- It can be utilized *without leaving your home* and makes for great rainy day or evening activities.
- It can allow you to *communicate* with other parents who are raising their children bilingual, regardless of where you (or they) live.

tool. In fact, many schools today expect students to use a computer to complete homework assignments and write papers. So, some experts believe it makes sense to extend total daily screen time as long as it's for a specific, educational purpose.

In the case of second language acquisition, the Internet, MP3 downloads, educational computer games, TV, and videos and DVDs, are a virtual gold mine, because they can provide a near endless stream of language exposure for your child. And because it's entertaining, kids aren't as apt to notice that they're "working" at language acquisition.

The Internet

The World Wide Web has revolutionized our access to resources, information, and other people. As a result, it has made it easier to raise a bilingual child, especially if you live in a predominantly English-speaking area that offers few local bilingual resources.

Before the Internet, parents who wanted to purchase foreign-language learning materials, particularly for languages other than French or Spanish, were often out of luck. Now, with just a click of the mouse, it's possible to purchase a wide variety of materials in dozens of languages from online retailers such as "World of Reading" (www.wor.com).

The Internet of course offers loads of free resources, too. Most radio and television stations have Web sites, and doing a search for those that serve the country that speaks your chosen language can produce rich dividends. These Web sites often offer fun and educational activities for kids of all ages, from preschool on up. (For example, www.rai.it, the Web site for *Radiotelevisione Italiana,* offers activities for kids in Italian.)

One advantage to Web sites that are affiliated with television stations, even those in other countries, is that their activities often feature characters from TV shows that your child is already familiar with. This can really help, especially initially, to engage and motivate your child. You might be surprised at how universal TV shows are. There are now 20 international editions of *Sesame Street,* and most animated shows have now been dubbed into other languages. Don't forget to look closer to home, too. An integral part of *Dora the Explorer,* a TV show for preschoolers on Nickelodeon, is simple Spanish language instruction. There are many accompanying activities on www .nickjr.com.

Generally, the activities on these sites are updated frequently, even daily. Some offer a "story of the day" or a "weekly adventure." Additionally, the activities are tailored to the developmental level of the children they are intended for. So typically, the activities for three-year-old children are designed so that they do not depend on reading. (The directions are spoken and at most, children have to recognize letters, symbols, or numbers.) If your child has had limited input in your language, he may want to start out with the activities that are geared toward kids a little younger, and that's just fine. The important thing is not so much the game or activity itself, but that he's listening to the directions, the songs, and the "you are right, the correct number is five!" in the second language.

Don't totally dismiss noneducational Web sites out of hand. There may be some angle you can work to your child's bilingual benefit. The "Kids of the World" section of the Kids Online Resources Web site (www.kidsolr.com/kidswww) offers one-stop shopping for kid-related (as well as educational) Web sites in an array of languages, from Portuguese to Korean.

Also, educational Web sites that are available in your language can add language input, even if their focus is not on language instruction per se. For example, www.mathstories.com offers math instruction in Spanish!

As the possibilities of Web resources are literally endless. I recommend that you spend some time surfing. If you Google words in your language that describe the type of activity you're looking for, then chances are that a plethora of interesting Web sites will pop up in your language too. First try the sites out yourself, and if you like them and your child enjoys them, bookmark them under your favorites. Be sure to incorporate visits to them into your weekly bilingual schedule. (A worksheet at the end of this Step will help you map out your schedule, day by day.)

Keep in mind that your child doesn't necessarily have to do all the activities while online. For example, you might print out the story of the day and read it at bedtime.

Older kids of course, like adults (or perhaps even more than adults!) use the Web to get information. Few kids these days look up a topic in a traditional encyclopedia—in fact fewer and fewer families even *own* a multivolume set of encyclopedias. As a habit, or "language boundary," you could consider telling your child he needs to look up information on the Internet in your chosen language. Wikipedia, for example, can be logged on to in multiple languages. (However, because anyone can add to or edit Wikipedia's content, it should probably not be relied upon as a definitive source.)

Downloading MP3 podcasts off the Internet is becoming increasingly mainstream and an integral component to language learning. Free daily Mandarin Chinese podcasts, for example, are available at www.chinesepod.com. The wonderful thing about podcasts, especially for parents who are not fluent in the language, is they provide input from a native speaker.

Another huge advantage to the Internet is it allows you to communicate with other parents raising bilingual children regardless of where you (or they) live. Web sites such as www.multilingualchildren .org and www.bilingualfamiliesconnect.com, enable you to reach out to other parents who have undertaken the same journey that you have.

Educational Computer Games and High-Tech Toys

In the past few years, educational computer software programs have faded into the background a bit as Game Boys, PlayStations, and

Xboxes have taken over the scene. But educational computer games in your language, such as those that emphasize reading, counting, and listening to stories can be a great way to increase your child's language input. Computer games are another language acquisition activity that your child is unlikely to object to. Furthermore, you can tailor programs so they match the proficiency level of your child.

As with DVDs, Rosemarie only buys computer games that can be played in French. When Rosemarie's younger daughter Vivianne was a preschooler, she loved a computer game based on the Madeline books. The rule, though, was that she had to click on the French flag at the beginning of the game. As a result, "Vivianne learned to count in French before she could in English," Rosemarie says.

There are interactive educational toys that can support your bilingual efforts, too. Leap Frog, for instance, offers a "bilingual learning collection" with interactive products that teach children concepts in English and Spanish. As with computer games, your child won't even realize he is learning while playing!

Television

It doesn't occur to most us to consider the TV as a source of second language input, yet most cable companies offer access to foreign TV channels, if not in their basic package, then for a small additional monthly fee. Companies don't often advertise this, but it is easy to call up and ask for their listings. If you already have cable, this can be an inexpensive way to get extensive language input for your children and yourself. If you don't have cable or access to channels in your language, an array of international TV channels are available via Web sites such as www.iTV.com, or www.beelineTV.com.

Parents often wonder if TV can actually help teach kids language skills, as opposed to simply providing language exposure. Recent research has shown that *Sesame Street* and *Between the Lions,* two quality programs for young children on PBS, enhance language development in general. And *Arthur,* another PBS show, has been shown to support language development, specifically in Spanish-speaking children who were learning English.

Radio

In today's visually driven world we often forget that the radio is also a source of information and language input. Depending on where you live, you may be able to tune into broadcasts in a foreign language. Web sites of public radio stations in different countries also offer "live radio." These programs can be especially helpful for adults trying to improve their language skills or reconnect with another language.

Videos and DVDs

When Amy was pregnant with her son Jeremy, she and her husband Jack decided they would speak to their child in German and learn German along with him. (Up until that time they both only spoke English.) "Jeremy was born in the days of videos," Amy says, "and his first video was *Teletubbyland,* in German. He watched it until it broke—literally. Until he was a preschooler, he thought that the TV only played videos, and videos were only in German!"

Videos and DVDs are perfect for younger children, who tend to love one show, in particular, and like Jeremy, love to watch the same story over and over. Happily for parents who are raising their children bilingual, many DVDs bought in the United States come in multiple languages. Some parents let their kids watch the DVD once in English to enhance their understanding of the story and then switch to the second language for subsequent viewings. Other parents opt to watch the DVD along with their child and pause it to explain what's going on if the child has trouble following the plot. One note of caution: If you buy international DVDs, make sure they'll work with your DVD player. Most international DVDs require a "zone-free" player.

"Old-Fashioned" Activities

I refer to these activities as "old-fashioned" because they don't require a computer, television, or DVD player (!) and also because they're "tried-and-true" activities that children have been enjoying—and learning from—for generations.

Young children love nursery rhymes and songs, and they are wonderful from a linguistic point of view. They expose children to lots of words, expressions, and perhaps most important of all, to rhymes. When it comes to language development, rhymes are important because they help train the ear to listen for and learn to identify subtle differences between similar sounds. Mastering the sounds that similar-yet-different combinations of letters make in a given language is an essential component of learning to speak, read, and write in that language.

If you prefer that someone else lead the singing, sing-along CDs or cassettes offer a true feast for children, as well as a major developmental boost. And also available are CDs or cassettes with an accompanying picture book. Being able to look at the words as they're being spoken or sung, as well as at pictures that illustrate the words, makes the experience a little more interactive and even more compelling for the child. Also, you don't have to be as concerned about whether your child comprehends all the words. The book's pictures will help him understand that, say, Humpty Dumpty is sitting on a wall, and that "le Pont d'Avion" only goes half way and that people dance on it.

A quick word here about books. Even though technology's bells and whistles can help "sell" language-building activities to kids, none of the activities I've mentioned should be considered a replacement for reading. Reading to your child in your chosen language (and later, having him read on his own when he reaches that level of language proficiency) is a remarkable booster for language development, and it is a bottomless well for language input. I will speak extensively about literacy and tips on how to read to your child in Step 6.

Finally, try to look at any fun activity you do as a family as an opportunity for language input. For example, if you are going to the beach, you could get a picture book about the sea from your local library before you leave and go over ocean-related vocabulary. Your child will be excited about going to the beach, so his interest in learning the words will be heightened. One of the biggest challenges you'll face as a bilingual coach is making repetition interesting, so try to take advantage of any opportunity, like a trip, that offers multiple ways to reinforce new words. For example, after introducing the ocean-related words, you can practice them while you're at the beach, and then after you get home, write captions for your pictures that include words.

Part Two: Making the Most of Community and Family Resources

Most parents who are raising their children bilingual (myself included!) are reassured to find out that achieving bilingualism does not have to be (and in all truth, probably cannot be) solely an "in-home activity."

Your Friends and Neighbors

While brainstorming with other parents who are raising their kids to be bilingual is an obvious, and often tremendous, source of support and ideas, don't be shy about sharing your bilingual goals with the people in your life. Discussions with other parents, your child's teachers, your friends, neighbors, and colleagues, regardless of whether they are monolingual or bilingual (or even whether they could imagine speaking another language other than English to their own children), can sometimes be surprisingly helpful toward finding new ideas to add to your Bilingual Action Plan.

Your Local Library

Whatever your chosen language might be, visit your local library. You might be pleasantly surprised at the collection of foreign-language books and resources available. Also, many people are unaware that they may request that their library purchase specific books and materials. Your library might not buy a whole stack of books just for you, but they might agree to buy a few children's books in a second language, especially if you and another family make the same request. Also, many libraries have a reciprocal lending arrangement with other libraries, and you can borrow books from those libraries free of charge. As librarians themselves say "Ask your librarian for help." Libraries contain a world of information, and it's often a much larger world than we realize.

Your Babysitter

As Jennifer, whose serendipitous hiring of a Mandarin-Chinese speaking babysitter led to her three daughters becoming fluent in Mandarin can attest, a babysitter who speaks your chosen language should be seen as a pearl. Many parents who are raising their kids bilingual already know that, of course. Katya told me, "We live in a college town and I bumped into Irena, a college freshman, at our community holiday party. As soon as she told me she spoke Russian, I asked her on the spot if she could babysit for us. In the beginning, she babysat one afternoon a week. She connected with the kids and our family straight away. By her senior year, she was babysitting between two and four times per week. I know that my kids would not speak Russian as well as they do today if she hadn't been there. I got very lucky, but my advice to parents is to take extra time to search far and wide for a babysitter who speaks your language, because it can make such a huge difference."

It can indeed. If your babysitter speaks your chosen language, it can add hours of language exposure each week. Equally important, it increases the importance of the language in the eyes of your child. If at all possible, ask your babysitter to speak the language (and only that language) to your child from the beginning. This creates a straightforward language boundary for your child.

Your Extended Family

If you have extended family members nearby who speak your chosen language, visiting them and encouraging them to speak the language with your children is invaluable. But don't automatically assume that your parents or in-laws (or any other family members) will be an integral part of your Bilingual Action Plan. Typically, there are also other grandchildren who want and need their grandparents' care and attention, and your siblings or brothers- and sisters-in-law may be raising their children to be monolingual in English or to speak different languages than the one(s) you're teaching your kids. So, communication is critical. Let your family members know that you are raising your child bilingual and that this is important to you, in no small part because you want to pass on your family heritage, and that you need and appreciate their help in this endeavor. Specifically ask them if they will support you in your goals, and if they will speak to your children in their language and pass on their heritage.

Be aware, too, that as your child enters preschool or kindergarten he might try to get these family members to start speaking to him in English. Rest assured, this is completely normal from a development point of view, and I will delve into it more and suggest strategies for dealing with it in Step 5, but I'll say here that it can be extremely helpful to give your family members a "heads up" that this might occur. Realize that grandparents, especially, can feel torn when their grandchildren ask them to speak in English. They want to please their grandchildren, even if they are also proud of and attached to their heritage. So, have compassion for their feeling caught in the middle, but remain firm with them (and with your child) as to what is acceptable to you.

For some, family gatherings mean having to travel to another state, or an even greater distance. The effort is well worth it in terms of the beneficial effect such a trip can have on your child. As I have emphasized throughout the Step, one of the key ingredients for achieving bilingualism is identifying positively with the chosen language. When a child gets to spend time with his extended family, all of whom are speaking "his" language, it increases his sense of belonging and worth.

Your Travel

Any bilingual parent who has visited his country of origin—or monolingual parent who has visited the country where her chosen second language is spoken—knows it is an irreplaceable experience. For a young child, such a visit can be the first time he hears the language *he* speaks being spoken by people outside his family. And like young Katherine who on her first trip to Greece told her dad, awestruck, that "all these people speak Daddy's language," it can be the first time your child realizes that he shares a language not just with his family members, but with thousands, if not millions, of other people. Furthermore, the effect of immersion can sometimes be stunning. A few weeks in France, Cecilia reported, and her son "was carrying on entire conversations in French."

Even if you don't have an immediate tie to the country where your chosen language is spoken, that doesn't mean you can't form one. For instance, when Darlene, an elementary school teacher who spoke only English, adopted a baby girl from China, she thought it was important that her little girl, Lily, maintain a connection to her heritage. So she placed Lily in a daycare center run by a Mandarin-speaking family. Through the daycare center, Darlene discovered that her town in the United States and a school district in China had developed a teacher-exchange program. Darlene signed up for it, and she and Lily spent a year living in China and learning Mandarin!

No Community Support Where You Live? Create Some!

Raising a bilingual child in the United States is, to use a distinctly American expression, a long row to hoe. Support is crucial, and necessary. In this situation, "divide and conquer" is not the best strategy, but rather, "l'union fait la force" (unity is strength) is.

So, wherever you live, make a concerted effort to find other families who speak, or are learning to speak, your language. The level of their language abilities or the age of their children doesn't really matter. You just want a group that can get together to speak the language, exchange ideas, share resources, encourage each other, and if there is a teenager present, perhaps even get a great babysitter who can also add some extra language input! If forming such a group seems daunting, consider that it really isn't any more complicated than starting a book club.

For younger children, play groups can be ideal. Try to keep up a regular schedule, like the first Monday of the month, or the second Thursday. At some point you may want to formalize the language learning aspect, and perhaps hire a group tutor.

Part Three: Finding School Support

7 Reasons to Consider Adding a School Component to your Bilingual Action Plan

1. *It can help motivate your child.* Being with other children who are learning the same language can be very motivating. (I know I sound like a broken record by now, but motivation

is absolutely essential to learning and to sticking with your goals!)

2. *It can give you support.* You will meet other parents who are undertaking the same journey, and together you can celebrate the accomplishments and help each other overcome the obstacles along the way. Your child will also undoubtedly develop strong friendships with other children who attend the school.

3. *It can provide a sense of community.* You will be part of a larger group that is working toward a common goal.

4. *It can take some of the pressure off you.* As I've said, being a parent/teacher/coach isn't always easy. It can be helpful then, not to mention comforting, to have another person—the teacher—there to shoulder some of the responsibility. The teacher creates the curriculum, prepares the materials, and does the actual teaching. An added bonus: The teacher (not you) is to blame for homework!

5. *It can expose your child to a native speaker.* Especially if you're not fluent, this is a great opportunity for your child to get language exposure from a native speaker who speaks fluently and without an accent.

6. *It can enhance "in-home" learning.* What goes on in the classroom can spark ideas or the teacher herself may suggest fun ways for increasing language exposure at home and reinforcing the learning that goes on in the classroom. For example, if your child especially enjoys a character in a book that the teacher uses, you could ask if there are other books of the same series. Or, if your child is learning the months of the year and the days of the week in school, you could work on the same vocabulary words at home, and add the challenge of learning to spell them.

7. *It can encourage and facilitate your language learning, too.* Often, monolingual parents of children enrolled in the school will get together and set up language tutorials for themselves.

In Step 6, I discuss in depth reading and writing in a second language and, then, in Step 7, I present various academic settings and how they support (or undermine) bilingual families. But I'd like to start by familiarizing you with various school scenarios that can support your family's bilingual goals. Many families start out thinking that raising their children bilingual will require enrolling them in a full-time bilingual school, but the truth is that most private bilingual schools are prohibitively expensive. Below are some alternate solutions that can be a great compromise and successfully support your bilingual goals.

Public Schools

First, the good news. Public school systems nationwide are offering ever-growing foreign language programs, starting as early as kindergarten. The Center for Applied Linguistics' most recent National Survey of Foreign Language Instruction in the United States estimates that 31% of elementary schools now offer foreign language instruction.

Now, the not-so-good news. Unfortunately, these programs have shortcomings, especially for parents looking to them as a cornerstone for their Bilingual Action Plan. Even though the array of languages offered continues to increase, Spanish and French remain the most common languages taught in elementary schools. This sends many parents who are interested in another language back to square one.

Additionally, in these second-language classes, children who already speak the language are often placed with students with no prior exposure to the language. This can be problematic for children who have been learning the language since birth or preschool because the classes can quickly become repetitive, even boring. For them, not only is it questionable whether the classes can help them progress, but there's a risk that their boredom will decrease their motivation to learn the language. On the other hand, if your child is first exposed to a language in an elementary-school course and has fun learning some expressions, it can spark his interest in continuing to pursue the language (and your interest in having him pursue it) and can serve as a good stepping stone to the next level.

But be aware that these programs are rarely designed to support the kind of long-term study that is necessary to reach fluency in the second language. In fact, foreign language instruction in most public school districts in the United States will probably not be enough, in and of itself, to develop solid bilingual skills. But the foreign language teachers in your child's school might be helpful in finding further resources.

Saturday or Sunday Language Schools

These are very popular throughout the United States and have successfully taught languages to generations of children. Many such schools are not for profit and have very reasonable tuitions. They often receive financial support from the country or countries where the language originated. As a result of their popularity, however, there is often a waiting list. So if this option interests you, I recommend looking into it sooner rather than later in case there will be a wait time before your child can enroll.

I also strongly recommend finding a school that is serious in its mission to teach language and culture. In other words, absences are counted, late arrivals are not appreciated, and children are assigned homework and are expected to do it. If you and your child are getting up early on Saturday or Sunday morning, and your child is going to miss out on other activities to learn Japanese, for example, then it should be worth your while. And it certainly can be. Many students who attend these schools take an AP (Advanced Placement) test in their respective language and score high enough to earn college credit. (You can find more details about AP tests at www.college board.com.)

At-Home Tutoring

Karen and Jeff are monolingual and are home-schooling their three children. Their school curriculum includes Spanish. Because Karen and Jeff don't speak the language themselves, they hired Adelina, who is fluent in Spanish, to come to their house and tutor the children. Karen found Adelina through an ad she placed at the local college. "Adelina not only speaks with the kids in Spanish, but actually teaches them following the curriculum we set up, assigns them homework, and corrects it," Karen explains.

Isabella, on the other hand, hired a Spanish-speaking tutor for a different reason—and with different expectations. She wants her son, Carlos, to be able to carry on a conversation in Spanish, the language of her heritage. Because Carlos has attention deficit issues, Isabella thought that a tutor, who would work with him one on one, would be better fit than a formal class. So Isabella found a retiree to spend an hour each week chatting with Carlos in Spanish. "She is very affordable and she comes to our house which works well with my hectic work schedule," says Isabella. "Plus, she speaks at his level and about anything that he's interested in, so it's fun and nonthreatening for him."

As you can see from the two scenarios above, a tutor has many advantages, not the least of which is that he or she usually comes to your house at a time that is convenient for you. And often the service can be surprisingly affordable. The downside, parents who go the tutor route relate, is that unlike with a Saturday or Sunday school, you have to organize everything from scratch. But, with a tutor, you do get to specify your language goals and how your child learns best—a degree of say you're not likely to have in a school or any other group learning setting.

If your goal is a high proficiency level, your child might require a more experienced tutor, who can be more expensive. But Karen discovered an ideal solution: a college student. Most colleges have listings of students who are interested in earning some money through tutoring. The listings indicate the students' majors, the languages they speak, and their tutoring experience.

"Do-It-Yourself" Language-Learning Programs

There is no shortage of a "do-it-yourself" foreign language courses to choose from. Many frequently recommended programs use interactive computer components, typically either CD-ROMs or online downloads. They include, but are certainly not restricted to, Rosetta Stone, The Learnables, Power Glide, Transparent Language, and Tell Me More. When choosing a program, keep in mind that children have different learning styles. So, while a particular program might work wonders for one child, it might not for another. Also, it sounds obvious, but do make sure the program is age appropriate. A program whose target audience is high school (or adult) foreign language learners may not be the best choice for your kindergartner. And before buying any program, be sure to do a little homework to determine if it meets your bilingual goals, your schedule (look at the amount of daily instruction time recommended), and your preferences for *how* your child receives instruction. For example, if you prefer a "manual" approach (textbooks, workbooks, and so on), you might not want a program that requires 30 minutes of exercises on the computer *and* listening to a story on the computer each day.

Foreign-Language Summer Camps

If you are planning to send your child to summer camp anyway, you might want to consider a camp where your language is spoken.

Although sleep-away camps abroad are generally an expensive way to get language instruction (for the same amount of money, you could get many hours of at-home tutoring), they do offer a tourist and cultural component, which can certainly be attractive.

Camps within the United States that specialize in teaching foreign languages are generally more affordable than those abroad (for one thing, you're not paying for an international flight), with prices that may be comparable to other sleep-away camps you're considering. And these camps tend to offer the usual range of camp activities, such as arts and crafts, outdoor pursuits, and various sports, on top of language exposure. As far as language learning goes, you can expect that your child will receive at least a certain amount of ongoing input, because in most instances the camp staff is required to speak only in the foreign language, but be aware that in reality, a lot of English gets spoken, too, especially when kids talk among themselves. Some camps, however, do offer the option of intense language instruction, which can range from a few hours per day to rigorous AP exam preparation.

Part Four: How Three Families Are Raising Bilingual Children

I want you to meet three families with different backgrounds and different bilingual goals and then check out their weekly bilingual schedules (as well as some advice from me as to what they might do differently). I hope you might be able to relate to some of these situations, and adopt some of their strategies for your own. One final bit of advice that I give to all families is to continue to adapt your family's weekly Bilingual Action Plan as your children grow (I will speak about this in Step 7). This may sound obvious but you'd be surprised how easy it is, once you're in a routine—and it's great to have a routine—to stick with it, even for years. So make a point of periodically revisiting and revising your Weekly Bilingual Action Plan.

Stephen, Elsie, and Sophia: OPOL Plus Variation of OPOL

Stephen is a second generation Chinese-American. His wife, Elsie, is monolingual English speaking. They have a two-year-old daughter, Sophia. Stephen and Elsie are both surgeons and work long hours. Stephen's parents take care of Sophia much of the time, and they always speak Mandarin-Chinese, their native language, to their grand-daughter. "Both Elsie and I want our daughter to be bilingual, but we know that in order to make that happen she needs a lot more language input than I would be able provide, at least right now," Stephen told me. "Also, I have to be honest. With our brutal schedules, Elsie, Sophia, and I have precious little time to spend together as a family and sometimes I don't always end up speaking Mandarin to Sophia during that time. It seems easier to speak English, especially knowing that Elsie doesn't understand a word of Mandarin. However, when I filled out our weekly Bilingual Action Plan (Figure 4.1), it really made me see that my parents were doing all the 'work', and I'd like to change that."

The expert suggests:

"When I answered the question 'how important is raising your child bilingual to you?' (Worksheet 2 on page 49) I wrote down an eight (out of ten)," Stephen shared with me. However, as he himself noted it is quite clear that he is depending on his parents to pass on something that is really important to him.

My advice to Stephen on changes he could make right now:

- Before trying to move forward, Stephen should back up and *talk with Elsie about how important it is to him that Sophia be bilingual.* It is never too late to have this discussion, and it can make a huge difference. More often than not, when partners are pulled in and begin to feel included in the process, they

FIGURE 4.1

Stephen, Elsie, and Sophia's
Family Weekly Bilingual Action Plan

Write in the *activities, who* will do them, and what *materials* will be needed. Try to space the activities evenly throughout the day and the week (if possible with at least one activity every day).

	Monday	Tuesday	Wed	Thurs.	Friday	Saturday	Sunday
a.m.							
Midday	Sophia spends all these days with my parents, who only talk Mandarin-Chinese with Sophia.						
Afternoon							
Evening							

become *part of* the process. Having both parents "officially" on board and equally invested in helping their child become bilingual is crucial for the long term.

- *Encourage Elsie to learn the basics of Mandarin.* She doesn't have to start with the goal of becoming fluent (although adults can and do achieve fluency in a second language). It is often better, anyway, to set an initial goal that you know you can reach. That way, you're more likely to get going, and achieve the success that will keep you going. A good initial goal for Elsie right now, and one which won't require a big commitment on her part, might be to pick up enough conversational Mandarin to understand what Stephen is saying to two-year-old Sophia.

- *Stephen shouldn't beat himself up because he hasn't been speaking consistently to Sophia in Mandarin up to this point.* Sophia has been getting hours of language input in Mandarin from Stephen's parents since her birth, which is great. And Stephen can take comfort in the fact that the times when it will be most crucial for him to support Sophia's Mandarin skills, such as when she transitions to preschool and then to school, are still ahead. Oftentimes the most difficult part of speaking to your child in a second language is simply starting. So I recommend Stephen start by taking *one small step that he feels he can do successfully.* For instance, Stephen might speak Mandarin to Sophia every time he picks her up or drops her off at his parents' home. This should be quite easy as Sophia is used to speaking Mandarin in this environment and his parents will be speaking Mandarin too. Once he becomes comfortable doing that, he can slowly extend his speaking to Sophia during other activities at home, such as reading a storybook to her in Mandarin on the weekends.

Mike, Jane, James, and Emily:
Monolingual Family Becoming Bilingual Together

"I took a couple of semesters of Spanish in college," says Jane. "But within a few months of the class being over, I could hardly speak a word of Spanish! Mike never learned a foreign language. About five years ago, we decided we wanted our kids, James, who is now 9, and Emily, who is 7, to have a different experience. We also decided that it wasn't too late for us to learn a language, either! Our bilingual goal for the kids (and ourselves) is to be able to speak and understand Spanish, but we want to keep the emphasis on having fun. Even so, when I went back to work full time a few years ago I was concerned that our language learning would just fall by the wayside. So I specifically looked for a babysitter who spoke Spanish. Rather than derailing our Bilingual Action Plan, my going back to work had the opposite effect: It encouraged me to find Theresa, whose presence in our lives has energized our Plan" (see Figure 4.2).

The expert suggests:

I told Jane that she and Mike are doing a great job. I applaud the fact that the two of them are taking a Spanish conversation class. It truly closes the circle and sends an important message to the children regarding the parents' commitment to the family's bilingual goals. Their weekly Bilingual Action Plan is impressive on two counts: It is filled with diverse activities and the activities are *spread out over the entire week.* Having daily input in a language makes it easier to learn that language. Daily input provides repetition and helps with memorization, two key components of language learning.

My advice to Jane on changes the family could make right now:

- Parents are often surprised to see how fast elementary-school age kids learn languages. By the time James reaches middle school, he is likely to be quite conversant in Spanish and will

FIGURE 4.2

Mike, Jane, James, and Emily's
Family Weekly Bilingual Action Plan

Write in the *activities*, *who* will do them, and what *materials* will be needed. Try to space the activities evenly throughout the day and the week (if possible with at least one activity every day).

	Monday	Tuesday	Wed	Thurs.	Friday	Saturday	Sunday
a.m.						Children's Spanish TV	Brunch in Spanish.
Midday							
Afternoon	Theresa, our babysitter for 4 years, speaks Spanish with the kids						
Evening	Spanish TV programs, the family watches DVDs in Spanish Wednesday evening Mike and I go to a Spanish conversation class						

probably be too advanced to get much out of Level 1 Spanish in middle school. It might be wise for him to start another foreign language at that point, so he won't be sitting in a classroom where the material being taught is far too basic for him. (I go over this situation in more detail in Step 7).

- Jane and Mike should consider reevaluating their bilingual goals for James and Emily. Time has been on their side. With the consistent Spanish input they have been getting over a period of years, they have a good chance of becoming quite fluent in the language. High schools often offer Advanced Placement Spanish courses, which could help them achieve this goal. However, to enroll in these classes James and Emily will probably need some reading and writing skills to go along with their speaking ability. Although reading and writing in Spanish may sound daunting, it's not really, especially for children who already have strong speaking and comprehension skills. (I discuss reading and writing in a second language in Step 6.)

Maude and Pauline: OPOL

"Although I've lived in the U.S. for years and speak English fluently, I'm from France," says Maude. "The first words I ever said to my daughter Pauline, when the nurse handed her to me in the delivery room, were '*bonjour mon ange*' (hello my angel), and I've spoken only French to her ever since (see Figure 4.3). I am a single mom and have been raising Pauline by myself. She's now 11. But a few years ago when Pauline started reading the easy words in our French storybooks by herself, I realized that I just wasn't up for teaching her how to read and write in French all by myself. It's one thing to help with homework, but being a full-fledged teacher is another. So I enrolled Pauline in a Saturday morning class at the Alliance Française. It hasn't all been smooth. Sometimes Pauline grumbles about having to get up

FIGURE 4.3

Maude and Pauline's
Family Weekly Bilingual Action Plan

Write in the *activities*, *who* will do them, and what *materials* will be needed. Try to space the activities evenly throughout the day and the week (if possible with at least one activity every day).

	Monday	Tuesday	Wed	Thurs.	Friday	Saturday	Sunday
a.m.	From the moment we get up Pauline and I speak in French.					French school	French homework
Midday							
Afternoon							
Evening	We watch the evening news in French on the TV together Evening reading in bed: alternates English and French books						

early on Saturdays or about the extra homework on top of her school-work. A couple of months ago her friends started taking a ballet class on Saturday mornings, and she really wanted to join them. It was hard for me to say no but I had to. I know how important it is that Pauline get consistent instruction and practice in French, especially because she speaks English all day long at school and with her friends. We're planning a trip to France later this year, though, and that made the ballet class decision easier on both of us."

The expert suggests:

Because of the OPOL method, Pauline is hearing and speaking French every single day (and has for years). This is obviously a great plus. Maude also wants her daughter to read and write in French. She deserves praise for developing, carrying out, and sticking to a plan that helps make this happen. It can be easy to put that decision off and as Maude said herself it's not always easy to stick to it, when kids complain about it.

My advice to Maude on changes she could make right now:

- Maude and Pauline started watching the evening news together because Pauline's social studies teacher in middle school wanted the kids to be aware of what was going on in the world. Maude saw this as an opportunity, and she signed up for the French channel through her cable company. This is great because both of them really look forward to snuggling up on the couch each evening and discussing the news. However, Maude should continue to keep an eye out for other activities in French that they can do together, especially as Pauline's needs and school schedule changes.
- The "tween" years are a great age for pen pals. With Maude's supervision, Pauline could consider corresponding in French with a girl her age in France. This is a great linguistic and cultural infusion.

- The upcoming trip to France is going to have a major effect on Pauline. She will visit where Maude was raised, and a lot of questions will be answered at many levels. However, because these trips are expensive, Maude should think about what the major goals of the trip are. What would she like Pauline to see and to learn? Maude and Pauline should discuss these goals before they leave, and do any preparation that will help Pauline get the most from the trip. For example, if they plan to see a play, they could read through it ahead of time. Maude should think, too, about how to make the effects of the trip last. Perhaps once they return home, Pauline can start speaking to or e-mailing her grandparents and other relatives in France on a regular basis.

Part 5: Create Your Own Bilingual Action Plan

Life coaches and productivity experts will tell you that one of the most effective ways to accomplish a major goal (and raising a child to be bilingual is a good example of a major goal) is to break it down into small, specific, and, perhaps most important, *manageable* tasks or activities that you can do on a daily or weekly basis. These experts also say that *writing down* these tasks and activities and actually scheduling them on our calendars makes it more likely that we will actually do them.

Worksheets 3 and 4 are designed to help you do both those things: one, to come up with the activities related to bilingualism that you want your family to do, and two, to schedule them. When you're finished, you'll have your *Bilingual Action Plan!*

93

WORKSHEET 3

What Are the Key Components to My Bilingual Action Plan?

Web sites

___

Internet activities

___

Educational software

___

TV programs

___

Video/DVDs

___

CDs/Audiocassettes

___

Books

Family activities

Community resources (friends and neighbors; local library; babysitter)

Extended family

Travel abroad

Public school

Saturday/Sunday school

At-home tutoring

Do-it-yourself language-learning programs

Foreign-language summer camps

Our Family's
Weekly Bilingual Action Plan

Write in the *activities*, *who* will do them, and what *materials* will be needed. Try to space the activities evenly throughout the day and the week (if possible with at least one activity every day).

	Monday	Tuesday	Wed	Thurs.	Friday	Saturday	Sunday
a.m.							
Midday							
Afternoon							
Evening							

97

5

Leaping over Predictable Obstacles

A s you progress along the road of raising your child bilingual, you may run into what I call "predictable obstacles." You might whiz right by them, or they may cause you to stumble a little. The goal of this Step is to let you know that they are there, so that you don't become discouraged if and when you encounter them, and instead, view them as expected challenges that can be surmounted.

In this Step, I'll discuss the *six most frequent obstacles* parents encounter and strategies for conquering them:

1. I'm not sure that I'm speaking to my child in a way that will help him to become bilingual.
2. My child does not want to speak my language anymore—she only wants to speak English.
3. My child keeps mixing languages.
4. I'm self-conscious about speaking my language to my child in public.
5. Because I'm the one who speaks a second language, I feel like I'm the one who is doing all the work to raise our child bilingual.

6. My work schedule has become really hectic, and there's little time for bilingualism.

Predictable Obstacle 1: I'm Not Sure That I'm Speaking to My Child in a Way That Will Help Him Become Bilingual

Parents raising their children bilingual regularly wonder if they are proceeding correctly. Parents will often ask me, "Is there a better way for me to speak to my child?" "How can I teach him new words?" "Shouldn't she be speaking longer sentences?" "How can I help him understand me?"

Child development seems to go in bursts and then to stop; but in fact, the brain is still learning.

This is important to know, because when the "slow downs" happen, it's easy for parents who are raising their child bilingual to become concerned that they're not "doing it right" and consider giving up on the idea of bilingualism altogether. Between 15 and 24 months of age, children tend to have an amazing vocabulary spurt. Parents rejoice as they see the speed at which their child learns new words. After this "surge" in learning new words, however, parents (even those who are teaching their child a single language, much less two) often feel that their child slows down, and they worry that she has stopped learning completely. "It was as if she was saying new words daily and then just stopped" is a lament I often hear. But child development specialists call this a plateau—a period during which the outside world might think that the child is not learning, but in reality, the child's brain is busy consolidating its newly learned skills. And two-year olds are not the only ones who experience plateaus. As your child continues to grow there might be other periods where you feel that he is not progressing in both languages, yet in fact he is, it's just less obvious. So, "keep on keeping on." The next language burst will soon come.

Once your child enters preschool, the language that's predominantly spoken in the country where you're living will probably become his stronger, dominant language. Your child can still progress in his first-learned language, and in fact his strong skills in his second but now dominant language can benefit progress in both languages.

As your toddler enters young childhood you may enroll him in preschool. From a language perspective, this usually means increased language input and a take off in his ability to speak the language used by his peers and teachers. As your child progresses through preschool, kindergarten, and elementary school, it is inevitable that the language he speaks at school and in the community will become his stronger language even if he has been speaking, and continues to speak, another language at home.

A shift in dominant languages can be a particular concern for parents who believe that as one language strengthens, their child's other language will weaken. Such a concern is not surprising given that even educators used to wonder if there was enough "space" in the brain to progress in two languages. But rest assured, there is.

As a parent, you *want* your child to develop strong English language skills—or strong skills in whichever language is the dominant language in your country—as these skills will be the basis for his academic, and later on, job success. In addition, you can take comfort in the fact that strong language skills in one language are "transferable" to another. For example, if you child is speaking in full sentences in one language (i.e., "I love snow storms because we then have snow days, and we get to play in the snow instead of going to school!"), then research suggests that she will strive to speak in full sentences in the other language. Similarly, your child's strong reading and writing skills that she is learning at school will help her when she picks up a book or writes a letter in her second language. (I will speak more about reading and writing in the second language in Step 6).

Q&A: *We've only spoken Vietnamese to our son, but he's about to enter an English-speaking kindergarten. To speed up his language development in English, should we stop speaking to him in Vietnamese and switch to English?*

The short answer is no. The longer answer is: It's not uncommon for parents who speak a language other than English at home to be concerned that their child might not pick up English fast enough once he enters school. This concern can lead parents to switch to English. But it is a myth that a child has to know English by a certain age to progress at school. Furthermore, developing strong skills in a language—any language—takes time. Dropping your language now will not accelerate your child's English proficiency. In fact, it might even impede the process, as it could detract from him strengthening his more complex language skills in Vietnamese. As discussed above, strong skills in one language aid in learning another. If your child has learned your language fluently and easily, there is no reason why he should not be able to pick up English in his school environment. (For more on this, see Step 3, "which parent speaks what language".) Continue to speak to your child in your language so he will continue to progress. His English will take care of itself.

There are things you can do to boost your child's language development.

How to speak to your child

As you know from the previous Steps, there is a direct correlation between language input and language learning. But, while talking to your child in your language sounds like a fairly easy thing to do, in reality it can sometimes feel challenging, especially if your

**9 Tips for *Speaking/Interacting* With Your Child
to Achieve Maximum Language Input**

1. Keep it *natural*. Everyday conversation is the best way for a child to learn.
2. *Keep on talking.* For example, on a rainy Sunday you might be thinking it's a pizza-and-DVD kind of afternoon. Think aloud in your language! You might say to your child in your language. "Does pizza in front of *Batman II* sound like a good idea to you? Where should we order the pizza from? What kind do you want?"
3. *You can talk, even if it is one way.* Even if your child is too young or not fluent enough in your language to reply to you, talk anyway! Studies show that children who hear a lot of elaborate vocabulary will also learn those words. For example, if you are preparing lunch, explain that you are mixing "mayonnaise" and "tuna fish."
4. Children *learn by doing* and any activity that uses one or more of their five senses enhances learning. So invite your child to get out the mayonnaise from the fridge and put some in the bowl and to smell the tuna fish. Showing her a picture of a tuna is great, too!
5. Use *gestures* to support what you are talking about and your explanations. Studies indicate that pointing and showing help children better understand and learn the meanings of new words. Researchers believe that pointing to an object helps a young child channel his attention and focus more intensely on what you are talking about. Gestures and pointing are especially important for younger toddlers, who do not have the expanded vocabulary needed to automatically understand what you might be talking about (the bee on the flower, or the airplane in the sky).
6. Give *context for the words* that you use. ("Tuna is a fish, like what you ate yesterday. Remember the salmon? That is another fish.")
7. *Try not to overwhelm* your child—a couple of new words at a time is fine.

Continued

8. It's fine to *repeat,* if you don't think your child understood what you said. And, in fact, even if your child *does* understand, repetition is necessary to reinforce the learning of new words. But as I've said before, do it naturally and as part of the conversational flow. (Remember, this is not a test!) You can also repeat and reinforce by saying the same thing a little differently: "You know the pink food we had yesterday with the potatoes? That is called salmon. Salmon and tuna are both fish. Fish swim in the water."

9. Even though your child is not always replying that does not mean that she does not understand you. *Remember that your child can understand more than she can speak.*

child is too young or not fluent enough to keep up a two-way conversation. These tips can help you talk to your child in a way that enhances language learning and stimulation.

Q&A: *Sometimes, despite repetition, my child still doesn't understand what I'm trying to tell him. Is it okay to translate some words?*

Translating may seem like the fast solution, but it can be like giving the answer away. Using gestures and pointing to objects or defining new words for your child using words he already knows keeps him in the mode of trying to "figure out" what you mean. Figuring out language seems to stretch and strengthen the brain in the same way that exercise stretches and strengthens a muscle, and many people think that this is one reason why bilinguals enjoy cognitive advantages. That said, there is some controversy regarding translating as a way to spurt understanding. The latest research shows that switching into another language *can* benefit the learning of new words. Translating target words can be an effective way to learn new words. But once again, it is important to keep the conversation fluid: "get me the ball, *pallina,* you know the red ball that we use to play soccer . . . ."

Keep in mind that occasional translating is not the same as constant mixing. Try not to mix languages constantly. Speaking your language without too much mixing will encourage your child not to mix. Plus, it will expose your child to a greater array of words in your language.

How to get your child to reply to you in your language

The other side of the language development coin, of course, is *getting your child to speak to you.* While you don't want to force your child to talk (remember that some children, like adults, are simply less talkative than others), you do want to be on the lookout for and seize every opportunity to converse naturally with your child in your language.

Q&A: *Is teaching body parts or similar drills useful in helping my child learn my language?*

The positive side of these kinds of drills is that your child will learn more new words in your language. And for the first few years, increasing vocabulary is what is going to increase your child's overall understanding of the language. However, it is important to keep in mind that learning a language is more than learning individual words; it's really about being able to take in and communicate information, whether by speaking, reading, or writing. So while it's fine to have a habit of teaching your child to count up to twenty, the days of the week, or even body parts, try to keep most of your teaching in context and in conversation. For example, if you and your child are in the car and a hot-air balloon passes by, and your child has never seen a hot-air balloon before, you could say "Hey, Juan, look at that on mommy's side, that's a hot-air ballon. A hot-air balloon is, . . ."

When your child *does* talk, how perfect should it be?

Parents often wonder how much they should correct their child and how much they should help her if she's struggling.

5 Tips for Encouraging *Your Child* to Chat

1. When your child asks a *question* (and as all parents know, children tend to ask a lot of questions!), it is a *golden opportunity* to encourage him to talk in your language. He'll be motivated to do so to get the information he wants.

2. If your child is *letting you know that she wants something* without actually saying so, such as pointing to a toy on a shelf, try to get her to talk. Ask her "What is it that you want?" (Even better, slip in more precise and more complex words, "You want something from the top of the cupboard? Which shelf, the top shelf?") If your child starts to get frustrated, just keep helping her out. ("Do you want the book? Do you want the paints? Do you want some more paper?") This exposes your child to more words in your language. And again, because she wants something, she is motivated to listen and attempt to answer you back.

3. *Kids like to talk about what they are interested in.* When you see that your child is engaged and enjoying an activity, encourage her to talk about it. Also, you can describe what she is doing to her. ("I love your picture, with the princess and her long blue gown.") Long descriptive sentences are super for learning.

4. *Elaborate on the activity that your child is doing in the moment.* Once again try to meet your child where he is at. For example, if you and your child are baking cookies, it's the perfect opportunity for a conversation. It is also the perfect chance to teach a new word (or two). You could say, "Here, why don't you crack the *eggs?* Or, "Would you please get me the *measuring cup?,"* versus just getting it yourself.

5. Talking to your child leads to *him* talking, of course, but so does *active listening.* While your child is talking, look at him and smile at him. This will encourage him to continue to speak. Acknowledge that you are listening by nodding and saying "Yes . . . really? . . . I didn't think of that!" and prompt him to continue ("and then what happened?" . . . "So when it started raining, did the game stop?")

- A good rule of thumb is to do what's needed to *keep the conversation flowing naturally* and your child talking. In other words, **don't** stop your child midsentence to correct her. And, if she is stuck on a word and you know what she wants to say, **do** go ahead and supply the word to help her along. If she says, "I want a, a, a, . . .". You can say, "A new battery?"

- Try to *replace words like "thing"* with the appropriate word. For example, if your child says, "I need a thing," while waving a dead battery at you, it's good opportunity to say, "Yes, let's go and get a new battery because that one must be dead by now." In this way, you both introduce the correct word and keep the conversation going. Also try to find a way to repeat the word, which is important for retention.

- Paraphrase what you child says and *add details* that will help your child use the correct idiom or "turn of phrase" in your language. This is how a child learns to say that a battery is "dead" versus "empty" or "broken" (both of which would be logical choices of words, yet are linguistically incorrect).

- When your child does talk with you, and does not mix languages, make a point to praise her for it. *Let her know that you are proud she can speak your language.* She will be proud too.

Predictable Obstacle 2: My Child Does Not Want to Speak My Language Anymore—She Only Wants to Speak English

In addition to the seven myths about bilingualism discussed in Step 1, another is that as children grow older they will automatically identify with the English language and refuse to speak another language. This is not necessarily so. But realize there are going to be times when your child's actions might make you think that is!

Annemarie, from Haiti, told me "When my son Jacques started preschool, I was told that he would try to start to speak to me in

English, and he did. But I have to say that even with the advance warning, I was taken aback and wasn't sure how to respond. Initially, I even stopped speaking to him in French and switched over to English myself. But luckily, it wasn't long before another bilingual parent told me that this was a normal developmental step and that I shouldn't give up or give in to Jacques. So I just kept on speaking French to him and redirecting him to speak it to me, and we were able to get back on track quickly."

Like Jacques, many children when they reach preschool or kindergarten age and begin to spend sustained periods of time in an English-speaking environment start to notice that many of their friends and their friends' families speak only English. Around that same time, a child's own English often starts becoming more fluent, too. The combination can result in a strong desire to speak English. But that desire is more of an expression of where your child is emotionally and developmentally than it is an intentional resistance to speaking your language. Understanding what is driving your child to want to speak to you in English makes it easier to see it as a predictable obstacle rather than a cause for alarm.

What's going on in my child's brain when this happens?

As I've mentioned before, the brain is naturally efficient, which means it strives to use the least amount of effort to get what it wants. For the bilingual brain that means using whichever language is the dominant one.

The key to counteracting this biological impulse, is, once again, consistency—both in terms of the language you use to communicate with your child and the language you expect your child to use to communicate with you. If you do that, your child will quickly learn that trying to speak to you in English is essentially a waste of her time and she'll be less likely to even try.

Even more important, consistency is what will ensure your child gets adequate language input—the key to gaining proficiency in a lan-

---

**3 Things to Do When Your Child Is
Not Speaking Your Language**

1. *Calmly redirect* her to repeat in your language.
2. Find *nonverbal cues* to let her know that you are not going to meet her request until she asks it in your language. "I just give Hannah my 'look' and she knows right away that she was speaking to me in English," one mom told me.
3. *Don't cave in if people around you express disapproval* or concern that you are "forcing" your child to speak another language. It can sometimes be difficult for a monolingual person to understand that raising a child to learn to speak two (or more) languages is in some ways like raising a child to learn to eat a healthy diet: You sometimes have to say, "You're going to eat a healthy snack instead of a candy bar."

---

guage. And as your child becomes more proficient in your language, her brain won't have to work quite so hard, and your child will become less resistant to using the language.

What's going on with my child emotionally and developmentally when she resists my language?

Parents often ask me (with one degree of irritation or another), "Why do I have to tell my child yet again why I want him to learn Punjabi?" Although it may *seem* like your child is asking repeatedly just to exasperate you, the truth is that at each new developmental stage, your child is taking stock of his world and working to make sense of it in the context of his higher developmental skills and his newly acquired knowledge.

So as your child grows, he examines his world a little more closely and with a little more complexity and, as a result, is often not satisfied with answers that may have satisfied him before. So even though you may have already patiently answered the question (more than once) of "why am I speaking a different language from my friends?" inevitably you will have to do so again—and in a more in-depth and complex way. This time around, for example, he might have questions about your family, where they come from, and if any relatives still live in the old country.

I've found that it is helpful for parents who are raising their children bilingual to know ahead of time not only that the question of "why" is going to be one that your child returns to again and again (call it a predictable hot topic!), but also to have a sense of your child's underlying motivation for asking it in the first place.

For instance, older preschoolers and kindergartners are becoming aware, for the first time, really, that while people and families share many similarities, they also are different from one another. So, at this age, your child is trying to figure out how families work, how other families compare to his family, and most important of all, how he fits in. In a nutshell, that's why this age group in particular is drawn to speaking English—they want to fit in. The tips on page 111 can help ease your child's anxiety.

Be forewarned that as your child grows older, his question of "why" may be framed in, shall we say, less-than-respectful ways. ("So we speak Armenian because Grandma's relatives died over there years ago.") It's easy to feel hurt or offended when this happens, but try to understand that underneath the impatience, sarcasm, and/or attitude, your child is as sincere about trying to understand why you speak your language and why you want him to as he was when he was younger. And the best thing to do is to try to answer him as patiently as you did when he was younger—and to be as steadfast as you were then in your expectation that he speak your language. Even if your child is not appreciative now, chances are he will be later. Remember, that even if your child might not seem interested, it remains important as ever to express pride in your culture and your language.

As Anna, who is a senior in high school, told me, "Sometimes I would be embarrassed that my parents would speak to me in Russian

**5 Ways to Help Your Preschooler or Kindergartner
Feel Good about Speaking Your Language**

1. *Help him understand and identify with your family's story.* Go over your family tree with your child, showing him the languages that each relative speaks.
2. Explain to your child in simple terms *why it is important and meaningful to you* that he learn your language and that you want him to continue to speak to you in your language.
3. Help him develop a *sense of pride* in his heritage and in his ability to speak your language.
4. Explain the "how" as well as the "why." *Familiarize your child with your family's Bilingual Action Plan.* ("Here's what Mommy and Daddy are going to do so that you can learn the language. To begin with, you and Daddy will continue to speak Greek . . . .")
5. If possible, *take your child on his first trip* to your country of origin. At this age, he is now old enough to remember it, and most likely, the immersion will lead to a language spurt and will help him identify with the culture. (See Step 4.)

in front of my friends. Then at some point, I kind of gave up that they would ever speak to me in English. I wrote about my bilingualism in all of my college applications. I realized that I'm proud to speak Russian, and proud of where I come from, and that I wanted to tell the world."

The road to bilingualism is going to have some bumps in it, in the form of disagreements between you and your child. He might even yell, "I hate you, and I hate your language." It goes without saying that this means that your child is upset. It does *not* mean, however, that he truly hates you or "your" language or even that the outburst could have been prevented if only your family was monolingual. (Even if you were, there would just be something else. Trust me.)

But as is the case with any disagreement, when this happens it is important to sit down and try to get to the bottom of what is really bothering your child and address it. If, for example, he's upset because he feels isolated when he speaks your language, try to make some connections with your extended family or with other kids his age that speak the same language or who are also bilingual.

Also look for opportunities to help your child share your culture with friends who come from different cultural backgrounds. For example, when you invite friends over for dinner, consider preparing a traditional dish for them. They surely will be interested and appreciative, and through this simple act you show your children you are open and proud of your identity, which makes it easier for them to be too.

"Our street is closed off to car traffic once a year for our block party," Jorge told me, "and for the past few years my family has prepared Tortillas for everyone. The first year we did this the kids were not so enthusiastic, but then they got one year's worth of compliments from all our neighbors. So now our whole family, including the kids, spends the whole morning before the block party cooking together. It is a great family experience, but each year I love seeing how comfortable they are with who they are."

Michiko told me, "As soon as my daughter entered kindergarten, I made a point to sign our family up to participate at the multicultural festival that the school holds every spring. We have a table where we demonstrate origami and where kids can make their own. My daughter gets dressed in a traditional kimono, and she always gets lots of compliments. I think this makes her feel proud of her origins."

One word of caution, however: If you find you're having continuous battles with your child over speaking your language, I do advise digging deeper. The second language may be a convenient scapegoat for other issues going on. For the most part, however, parent/child disagreements, including ones in bilingual families about speaking a second language, are a normal part both of growing up and raising children. The best thing you can do is to continue to talk with your children about why your language is important to you and why you want to share it with them. Studies show that children who feel proud of their heritage and their second language tend to embrace that language, and even say that they intend to "speak it to my own children when I have them."

Predictable Obstacle 3: My Child Keeps Mixing Languages

Understanding Language Mixing

Because there is so much concern about children mixing languages, I find that this is one of the most important aspects of bilingualism for parents to understand. The long-term goal, of course, is for a bilingual child to be able to speak without mixing languages, but mixing is part of normal language development, even for mono-lingual children, who, in the process of learning, frequently mix up words and different grammatical rules. Who hasn't heard a toddler call anything with wheels a "car," and what mother doesn't just melt when her kindergartner says, "Mommy, you are the 'bestest.'" In neither case does the child use correct English, but such mistakes are accepted (as they should be) as a natural part of learning of the language.

Researchers have not yet fully nailed down the complex brain mechanism that allows children to separate languages. But we do know that there is great variability among children as to when they start to do so. I always have a few parents who tell me, "My son never mixed at all. From the day he opened his mouth it was always either English or Hindi." In other words, mixing of languages and learning languages in general is similar to other developmental skills: Some children

113

might be more proficient in this particular area than others are, and will never mix languages. However, most children do, and it is considered to be quite normal.

Developmentally, as your child's brain matures, she will be better able to classify the words from both languages. At approximately age 2, she is aware she is speaking two languages, but most likely, she is not yet able to separate each of these languages. So a lot of words from one language might slip in while she is speaking the other. At about 3 or 4 years of age, most bilingual children start to verbally identify each language. They speak of "Mamma's language" or "school language." Some can even translate simple words. After that, children might still mix language traits, such as adding "i-n-g" (a typical verb ending found in English) to verbs in the other language or putting the words in sentences in one language in the order they would go in the other. But as their brains continue to mature, they typically become more efficient at separating the languages and using the correct words and grammar, and mixing them less. Learning and retaining new words, pronunciations, and grammar in two languages is a gigantic challenge for any child's brain. So it's no wonder that the separation process, even in a child who is bilingual from birth, can last well into mid-childhood. And as long as the mixing of languages is not actively encouraged, it usually disappears naturally about then.

When a child mixes languages, parents sometimes wonder if their child is just being lazy. But in fact, the opposite is true. In mixing, the dominant language is used to support expression in the less-fluent language, so the child is actually being quite efficient. He is using whatever way is necessary to make himself understood as quickly as possible. For example, a Spanish-speaking child in an English-speaking kindergarten may ask his teacher, "Where is the paint *rojo?*" if he can't find the *red* paint, in the hopes that she will tell him where it is so he can get on with what's really important, having fun painting!

That can sometimes lead parents (and other adults) to think that the child is confusing the two languages. But just because a child cannot immediately "find" a word in one language and then makes the decision to insert the correct word that he knows from another language, does *not* mean he's confusing the languages or that he's confused about which language that he's speaking. It's merely a matter of expedience. The child is doing whatever he can to get his needs met. In this way, the child is no different from a tourist visiting another country who generally makes a valiant effort to speak the language of that country, but is occasionally stumped as to what the word for something is. In this scenario, the tourist might go ahead and say the word in his native language in the hopes that his listener might understand it or at least be able to figure out what he is referring to. The fact is, bilingual children, like bilingual adults, don't speak full sentences in their language to a person who they know does not understand it. Even very young bilingual children will only speak a language that they hear a person speak, either directly to them or to some one else. (As we saw in Step 3, three-year-old Emmanuel never spoke Spanish or Portuguese to his English-speaking daycare providers.) If you stop to think about it, this is quite remarkable from a linguistic and social point of view.

Finally, it's also worth noting that monolinguals sometimes think a bilingual child mixes languages more frequently than he actually does. Because hearing two languages being mixed can be an unfamiliar sound to a monolingual, her ear "picks up" each instance of mixing. In reality, bilingual children speak more sentences *without* mixing than they do sentences *with* mixing. If a bilingual can formulate a sentence in one language without any mixing, he usually does so—with the exception of "code switching."

Understanding "Code Switching"

You may have heard of the term "code switching." It is not the same as language mixing, which serves a child while he is learning two languages. Code switching refers to switching from one language to

115

another to say individual words or parts of sentences. For example, when a child who usually speaks Italian with his father tells his dad to watch him turn on his skateboard, he might say: '*Andiamo Papa, voglio mostrarti sul* skateboard *come faccio* my new 180." The main reason he does this is because no kid in the world speaks about a "skateboard" and a "one eighty" (one-hundred-eighty degree turn) in a language other than English, especially if he knows that his father understands English.

There is an entire field of linguistic study devoted to code switching. Most bilingual children and adults (including balanced bilinguals) do it. As with most everything that has to do with language, code switching is a complex process. While research shows that a speaker might switch from one language to another when he does not remember a word in that language, it also shows that switching occurs when the speaker wants to emphasize a particular word or phrase. (A stereotypical version of this might be the satisfied, English-speaking chef who upon tasting his sauce smacks his lips and pronounces it to be "*absolument parfait!*") But switching is also very much tied to social circumstances and relationships. For instance, a bilingual might switch constantly with her best friend or siblings but not with her boss or coworkers. It's as if a bilingual person speaks two languages and then a third, a blend of the two that contains frequent code switching.

The bottom line is that bilinguals tend to think about language in a fluid, as well as a social and pragmatic way. The bilingual point of view is to use whatever language captures one's thoughts and feelings the best, and whatever language will be most appreciated by one's audience.

Is it okay then to let my child mix languages to her heart's content?

The short answer is a qualified no. The more complicated answer is you don't want to clamp down on language mixing too much because, as we saw above, it helps a young child who is learning two languages to express herself. But you also you don't want it to become a habit. Some adults have become so used to mixing that they cannot "find" certain words or even speak a full sentence in one language. And it's worth being aware that it's a habit that can develop easily and even unconsciously. Code switching can become so ingrained that bilinguals often do it without even noticing. So, if you are bilingual, try to be conscious of whether or not you are switching languages. As we've discussed, the brain always wants to take the easiest road. So if you are used to not "looking" for a wanted word in your language, but switch automatically into, say, English, and everyone you speak with does this, too, then it's more likely that your child will also develop this habit.

One might think that a child who is exposed to intense code switching will not be able to differentiate between two languages, much less learn both of them, but it is amazing how resilient children are when it comes to understanding different languages and not confusing them, even when they are blended. In other words, a child will not define the language spoken to him as being a new blended "English-Spanish" language, but will identify it as two separate languages. But that does not mean that he is automatically able to become proficient in those languages. As I've said so many times before, the level of language proficiency that a child can reach is directly tied to the amount of language that she is exposed to and the amount of practice she gets.

While the bilingual brain can flow naturally between separating languages and blending them for the purpose of communication and socialization, one of the best ways you can help your child develop proficiency in your languages and not rely on mixing or code switching as a crutch is to focus on not mixing yourself when you're speaking with her or when she can hear you speaking. For example, Melanie, who now lives in New York City, grew up in a bilingual environment

5 Dos and Don'ts for Handling Language Mixing

1. **Don't** correct your child every time she mixes English into your language.
2. **Do** keep the conversation fluid and natural.
3. **Do** offer positive reinforcement when she speaks a full sentence or takes a "new" step in your language. ("Wow, you said that all in Spanish, that's great!" or "I'm so proud of you for writing a letter to Grandma in Croatian. I know she will be too!")
4. **Do** repeat in your language the sentence in which she might have slipped in an English word. But don't call attention to it. Just do it in the flow of conversation. ("So you are asking if it is warm enough to go outside without a *jacket?*")
5. **Don't** respond immediately if she has switched into another language. Pausing and waiting for her to repeat herself in your language can serve as a nonverbal reminder that she has switched languages. By helping her become aware of when she does it, you can help prevent it from becoming an unconscious habit.

in Montreal. "Here in New York City, my friends from Montreal are all bilingual," she told me. "However, when I'm with them, they rarely speak even one full sentence in French or in English. Instead, they use a French-English mixture. But when I was growing up, my mother, who is an Anglophone, spoke to me in English and did not allow any mixing. 'English only' she would say. And to this day, I do not mix English and French. I speak one or the other."

Should I correct my child every time she mixes languages?

No, not every time. While it's true you want your child to learn your language and not an Anglicized version of it, it's important to keep the conversation natural, and not constantly interrupt and correct your child when she is speaking. Otherwise, you run the risk of discouraging her from even trying to speak your language.

Predictable Obstacle 4: I'm Self-Conscious about Speaking My Language to My Child in Public

For some parents this is never an issue. They use the One-Parent-One-Language strategy and always speak to their kids in their language, including in public. But for many parents this is a sensitive topic and one that can cause angst. Interestingly enough, it can also be the first predictable obstacle that you encounter, literally when your baby is in his stroller and you are taking him for a walk in the park.

Parents who are uncomfortable speaking their language in public will tell me that they want to do it *but:*

- "It makes me feel impolite."
- "It just does not come out."
- "When I am at the park and yell to my kids across the soccer field in Italian it feels as though I am the only one in the world raising her kids bilingual and that I am doing something really strange."
- "I'm not fluent, so when I speak to my kids in public I'm embarrassed. I'm concerned that someone is going to come up to me and correct my grammar or my pronunciation . . . although this has never happened."
- "When my husband speaks one language and I am speaking another, people turn around. We've even had complete strangers tell us that we must be crazy, or are confusing our kids."

I understand that all these reasons *feel* very real. Obviously, none of us wants to offend anyone by speaking in another language when we are at a social gathering. And clearly, we don't want our friends wondering if we're talking about them in a language they can't understand. And even though we don't necessarily feel the same degree of responsibility toward people we don't know, their judgments can still sting, even if they are way off base!

119

Take heart from Rosemarie, whom you met in Step 3. She is raising her two daughters, Simone and Vivianne, to be bilingual in French and English and, since their birth, she has been quite diligent about only speaking to them in French. But even so, she told me, at first whenever she and Simone were outside their home she tended to shift to English because she felt self-conscious. "I felt as though I was being impolite by speaking French when I knew that those around us didn't understand the language. But then when Simone entered preschool and her English was improving rapidly, she suddenly started answering me in English, even when we were at home. I realized then and there that I had to intensify the French side too, and I started speaking to her in French all the time, regardless of where we were. After a week or so she switched back to French. But it was a wake-up call. I simply started explaining to others that I speak French to my kids. Since doing that, honestly, I have never received anything but understanding and encouragement."

I realize, however, that simply making the decision to speak a language other than English outside your home and sticking to it is not so easy for everybody. Sometimes that's because beneath a superficial reason, such as wanting to speak English to be polite, there lies a more deep-seated reason that is often based in fear or shame. For example, a parent who grew up monolingual in English and is still learning another language herself might have an intense fear of being laughed at if she attempts to speak that language to her children in public. Conversely, a bilingual parent might worry that if she speaks her language of origin people will think she cannot speak English. And in a world that is sometimes suspicious of differences, a parent who was not born in the United States might worry that if she speaks a language other than English people will think she is not an American or assume that she is in this country illegally.

In fact, self-consciousness about speaking a foreign language in public is so common that parents frequently ask me, "Can't I just speak English to my child in public?" Again, because I understand that the fear or the threat of speaking a language other than English feels very real and because I want to encourage any parent to "go for" bilingualism whatever the circumstances, I say that if it's very uncomfortable, then that is what you should do. Yet, I also encourage parents to take an honest look at why it is so difficult and, if possible, to try doing it just once and see what happens. (There's a well-known self-help book entitled *Feel the Fear and Do It Anyway,* and I think that title sums up my advice in this situation.) You may find, as Rosemarie did, that people, or at least the people who really matter, are a lot more supportive and a lot less judgmental than you imagine they will be.

I also have to be honest: There are ramifications if you only speak your language to your child at home. As Rosemarie found out, where and when you speak your language suddenly becomes less clear cut for your child (and yourself). You also risk sending the message that learning the second language is not so important after all,

---

**3 Things You Can Do to Make
Speaking Another Language in Public Easier**

1. *Make sure your family, friends, and acquaintances know* that you speak another language with your children. If you're going to a party or event where the host might not know that you're raising your children bilingual, let her know ahead of time, and while you're there, mention it to other guests to alleviate any awkwardness.
2. Realize that people may have misconceptions about bilingualism and might not understand how it works. *Explain that maintaining consistency with the language is essential to mastering the language.*
3. Know that *unkind or judgmental comments are the exception.* The vast majority of people are very impressed to hear kids speaking another language and will compliment them. That kind of positive reinforcement can only help your child—and you!

---

which, as we discussed in Step 3 can deflate your child's sense of motivation and pride. Finally, it also really cuts down on the number of opportunities your child has to hear and to speak your language, which can impact the level of language proficiency she can reach.

But that said, remember, you are in control. *You* are the one who gets to decide when, where, and whether to speak your language or English, and you should make the choice that feels best for you and your family.

Predictable Obstacle 5: Because I'm the One Who Speaks a Second Language, I Feel I'm the One Doing All the Work to Raise Our Child Bilingual

You may have heard the African proverb, "It takes a village to raise a child." In my experience, as long as both parents are actively engaged in their child's life, it takes *both* of them to raise their child bilingual, even (and I might go so far as to add, *especially*) if one of the parents doesn't speak the second language. Even so, it is not uncommon for the parent who does all the talking to feel like he will be the one doing all the work or *is* the one doing all the work. But the chances of your child becoming bilingual are diminished considerably if your "non-speaking" partner does not support you and is not on board with the endeavor.

These scenarios illustrate how essential communication with your partner is to your child's bilingualism:

Example 1: Jamila, who speaks Arabic, told me, "I really want to raise our child to speak Arabic, but I haven't even broached the topic with my husband. He doesn't understand a word of Arabic, and I'm not sure how he'll feel if he can't understand what our child and I are saying."

Example 2: Rachel, a mother of three, is monolingual in English. Her husband is of Armenian heritage, and he speaks Armenian with his family members. "Every Sunday, my husband's family gets together for lunch," Rachel told me. "After awhile, I used the fact that I didn't understand Armenian as an excuse not to go. As our children got older, they started staying home with me. It wasn't until my husband pointed this out that I realized our children were missing out not only on their family traditions, but also on learning Armenian. I started going to the Sunday lunches again with the kids and I'm amazed at how quickly they resumed conversing in Armenian with their grandparents."

Example 3: Mirabelle came to see me because her husband Tom was convinced that she was confusing their daughter Nicole by speaking to her in French. Once I reassured Tom that this was not the case, his attitude changed. He started encouraging Mirabelle to consistently speak to Nicole in French, and he was the one to search for a French-speaking babysitter.

Keep in mind that it's not just open confrontations with your partner that can sabotage your bilingual goals for your child. If you haven't fully involved your partner in devising your Bilingual Action Plan, he or she can end up undermining it unintentionally. As we discussed earlier in this Step, most likely there will be points along the way when your child will try to speak to you in English and question why she "has" to speak your language. It is crucial to have your partner's support when you encourage your child to speak to you in your language and when you talk with her about why learning your language is important to you. As every parent learns, children naturally try to play off one parent against the other to get what they want, so if your child senses that your partner is ambivalent about this whole bilingual business, she will definitely try to take advantage of it.

Remember, too, that although talking with your child in your language is certainly a very big and very important part of teaching her that language, there are countless other tasks involved, such as gathering resources, perhaps finding a babysitter who speaks your language, dropping off and picking up your child from language school, and making sure homework is done. The list goes on, and you'll need your partner's help to do all of it.

It's also worth noting here that among parents who successfully raise their child to be bilingual, the parents who are the "language speakers" nearly always point out the close collaboration that they have had with their partner from the beginning and attribute the success equally. I can't tell you how many times I have heard statements such as: "I simply could never have done it without my wife;" "I will always be grateful to David for supporting me in this;" "We were both in it together;" "It was a family adventure."

Finally, you should know that if your partner is actively involved in your Bilingual Action Plan, the unappealing scenario, in which she doesn't understand the language and is either dependent on ongoing translation or is left out in the cold, doesn't occur that often —especially if you opt for the One-Parent-One-Language strategy and start talking to your child in your language at birth. When you do that, your partner has the opportunity to learn along with your child. And chances are, even if your partner doesn't plan on learning your language, she will pick up enough to understand what's going on.

Remember Anna and Frank whom you met in Step 1? That was their experience. "When Anna started to speak with our first child, Kayla, in Swedish, I was all for it, but didn't envision myself learning Swedish," Frank told me. "But to be honest, baby talk is not very difficult to pick up—especially for an adult. When I realized that I was 'getting it,' I was really proud, and it made me *want* to learn the language so I started to learn Swedish too. I've continued to speak to our kids in English, which is what we had planned all along, but when they speak to Anna in Swedish, I understand everything that is said!"

**4 Ways to Ensure That Your "Non-Speaking" Partner
Is Actively Involved in Raising Your Child Bilingual**

1. Recognize that *your partner's support and help* (or if you're divorced and your ex is actively involved in your child's life, his or her support and help) *is essential* to successfully raise your child bilingual.
2. Develop your family's bilingual goals and Bilingual Action Plan *in conjunction with your partner,* regardless of whether he speaks your language. Let him know that he will play an essential role, even if he never speaks a word of the language.
3. As you go along, *ask your partner to be your sounding board* and a reality check for your goals and Action Plan. (It's especially important to do this if your partner typically spends more time during the day with your child than you do.) How much time does your second grader *really* have to read in Hebrew each night? If the Hebrew language teacher says 15 minutes a day, does this work for your family?
4. If your partner is uncomfortable with some aspect of your bilingual plan, *don't dismiss or "overrule" her concern.* For example, she may be uncomfortable with the idea of you speaking your language to your child at a gathering of her family members. When an issue arises, be prepared to discuss it and try to find a solution that works for both of you.

Predictable Obstacle 6: My Work Schedule Has Become Really Hectic, and There's Little Time for My Child's Bilingualism

When your work schedule gets even more hectic than usual, it's easy to feel that there is simply not enough time in the day or week for your child's bilingualism and that it is one activity that can be put on hold.

But remember, that *when it comes to bilingualism, "later" often means "never."* So it is better—*much* better—to never stop completely. If you started to raise your child bilingual, it was obviously

125

Summing Up: 7 Things That Can Help You Continue on the Path to Bilingualism—Even When It Feels Like You Can't.

1. Create a *bilingual support system so you don't have to do it all yourself.* If your extended family speaks your language and is nearby, see if they can spend more time with your child. Or, consider finding a babysitter who speaks your language, hiring a tutor, or enrolling your child in a weekend language school.

2. Devise a diverse Bilingual Action Plan filled with *language-learning activities that do not necessarily require your presence.* For example, even if your partner does not speak your language, he can pop in a CD or DVD or supervise Internet activities in your language.

3. *Maximize* the time you *do* have to speak your language with your child by following the tips offered on pages 100 through 107, under "Predictable Obstacle 1."

4. Try to carve out *some special time each day to speak your language with your child.* If possible, make it a routine. Converse in your language each day over breakfast or dinner or read a book together in your language before bedtime.

5. Remember you *don't have to be face to face* to talk with your child. When you call him during the day, talk in your language, or if he can read your language, send him an e-mail or text message—and encourage him to write back in your language.

6. Remember from Step 2, it's very important to devise bilingual goals and a Bilingual Action Plan that suits your life *and* to *adapt* them as you go along to reflect changing circumstances. There's no shame in doing that. *What would be* a shame is to stop speaking your language with your child completely. Because in all truth, once you stop, starting to speak your language again is a true challenge.

7. Try to *avoid an "all or nothing" attitude.* I've seen some parents start out with the goal of balanced bilingualism and an equally ambitious Bilingual Action Plan and then if it becomes impossible to keep up that level of commitment, quit altogether. When life intervenes, don't give up on your dream of bilingualism for your child. Instead, simply *modify your plan, and if necessary, your goals.*

something that you really wanted to do. And I'm here to encourage you and to tell you, please do not give up now! If you do, you'll most likely regret it, because a child, or anyone, for that matter, who does not use a language will lose those skills very rapidly. Instead, draw on the tips in the previous Steps to help you formulate or modify your Bilingual Action Plan so that it can continue to work even when you're *at* work. (Some of the most useful tips for doing this are described on page 126.) Because when it comes to bilingualism, *something* is *always* better than *nothing!*

6

The "Two R's": Reading and Writing in Two Languages

You might wonder why you should embark on teaching your child to read and write in your language. After all, she is learning (or will learn) to read and write at school and there are many other activities competing for your child's time and energy (as well as your own). In this Step, I discuss the immense value of adding reading and writing skills to your bilingual goals for your child. And, I'll show you how to help ensure that your child develops these skills, even if he receives no instruction in your language at school.

Reading in a Second Language

Let's start with why reading in a second language is important:

1. Reading is powerful. Written material is considered by many to be the cornerstone of learning any language. Some linguists believe that reading alone can lead to the acquisition of a language. Indeed adults often base most of their learning of a foreign language on books. However, developing an oral understanding and an "ear" for a language first, and then progressing to reading it (the route that children usually take), offers two benefits: Oral language skills make it easier to progress in reading, and learning to read a language strengthens preexisting speaking skills.

2. Reading offers an additional and complementary kind of language exposure. Reading exposes a child to language at a "slow pace" compared to the "fast pace" of spoken language. Being able to look at and savor words and sentences for however long and for however many times he likes helps a child to process and learn a language.

3. Reading leads to increased vocabulary and better understanding, which in turn leads to greater facility and enjoyment when using the language. Reading is considered to be one of the main ways we are exposed to and learn new words in *any* language. The more words a child understands, the greater his understanding of the language in general. And the better a child understands a language, the easier it is for her to express herself in it and the more likely it is that she will want to use it.

4. Reading leads to higher level language skills. Learning to read a language is a giant step toward developing higher level skills in that language. Higher level language skills include not only the ability to formulate longer and more complex sentences but also the skills that are required to make sense of complex language, to problem solve in that language, and to be able to formulate and express oneself using more diverse and more precise vocabulary with greater efficiency. Once your child starts reading in your language you'll see her vocabulary and spoken language skills take off.

5. Reading leads to increased cognitive benefits. Learning to read in a second language is not only a significant step toward increased proficiency in that language, it is also a challenging brain workout. In short, higher level language skills promote higher level thinking. So, bilingual children who learn to read in two languages reap even more of the cognitive benefits associated with bilingualism.

6. Reading can help develop and safe-guard language skills over a lifetime. Solid reading skills in your language and a habit of reading books and other materials written in it enable your child to learn and enjoy your language with increased independence. And in the long run, being able to read in your language will enable your child to keep up his skills in that language even if later on, as a college student or as an adult, he no longer has an opportunity to speak the language regularly.

Reading in Two Languages: The Brain Can Handle It

You might be concerned that your child will become confused as he learns to read two languages because each language has different rules for the sounds that individual letters or groups of letters make (also called phonics). For example, in English "key" is the word for an object that is used to open a door, but in Italian the word "chi," which is pronounced nearly the same way, means "who." But again, give credit to the human brain. It is capable of distinguishing and remembering these differences astonishingly well.

But how does it work?

If you have visited a foreign country where you can't speak the language, you may have noticed that if the language is written in same Roman alphabet as English you can still "read" it, even if you have no idea what it is that you are reading. Someone who knows the language, however, might be puzzled by your strange way of pronouncing the words. In the same way that you use your reading skills in English to try to "sound out" a word in another language, a bilingual child uses his prior knowledge—his knowledge of the spoken language along with his developing reading skills in English—to try to guess at the printed words he sees. Only he has one advantage: He doesn't sound quite as funny when he says the words out loud!

In educational parlance, this is called the "transfer" of skills from one language to another. As we have discussed, language skills learned in one language, such as the ability to form long and complex sentences, are transferable to another. While it's true that every language has some reading rules that are specific to that language, core reading skills, such "sounding out" words by breaking them down into the smallest units (called phonemes), are also transferable from one language to another. So if your child is able to "decode" written text in one language then he will be able to do so in the other. Conversely, if he requires extra practice to read in one language, then chances are that he will also have to practice more in the other. (I will delve into this more in Part 2 of the next Step, where I discuss reading and writing difficulties and the bilingual child.)

But the exciting thing is that bilingualism, even at the spoken level, in and of itself appears to aid the reading process. Researchers have found that young bilingual children are better able than their monolingual peers to recognize the relationship between a letter and its sound (called letter-sound recognition), which is an essential "pre-reading" skill.

Even so, learning to read in two languages isn't easy

Chances are, your child is (or will be) starting to learn to read in your language about the same time he is in the process of learning to *read* in English and learning to *speak* more fluently in your language. That may seem like a lot for any child to handle, but in reality, the most challenging task at this level is learning enough vocabulary to be able to understand what you're reading and hearing and to be able to communicate what it is that you want to say in both languages. When a child who is monolingual is learning to read, he can pretty much focus solely on the process of reading, or "decoding," the written words on a page, because he understands what the vast majority of words in the text mean. However, for many, if not the majority, of children being raised bilingual in the United States, English is already their dominant language by early elementary school. So when they read a text written in their less dominant language, they not only have to work at decoding the written words, they have to simultaneously try to figure out what many of the words might mean.

From a practical standpoint this can make the reading process quite tiring for the brain. Oftentimes, after approximately 10 to 15 minutes of reading in the second language, a child who does not have a lot of practice reading in that language can be quite tired out.

Add this to the fact that when a child picks up a book written in his less dominant language he often must grapple with unfamiliar cultural references. For example, your child might not know automatically what a *paella* (a traditional rice dish) is, or *Fastnacht* (carnival festivities at the end of winter in cold central European countries), or *les vendanges* (picking of the grape vines in France). This might seem trivial, but many of these specific cultural references and events are often included in, or are even the theme of, children's books written in other languages. The same thing of course is true of countless children's books published in the United States. Many include mention of, or even revolve around, American customs and celebrations. It is fantastic for your child to be exposed to and learn about the touchstones of another culture, but keep in mind that it does add yet another layer of information for his brain to interpret.

Q&A: *As many language skills are transferable, can a child teach himself how to read in a second language?*

In the same way that a few children are able to teach themselves to read, some children are able to use their English reading skills to figure out the rules of written language in the other language. They might start off by picking up very simple books meant for pre-schoolers and, by using their reading skills in English, guess their way through the second language. But this is by no means a given. "We've raised both our daughters from birth to be bilingual in German and English," Gretchen told me. "Not long after our oldest learned to read at school in English she was able to pick up the simple picture books that I was reading to her younger sister, in German, and read them to her. But a couple of years later when our younger daughter learned to read in English, she was not able to automatically read in German."

Preschool/Kindergarten: Get Ready to Read!

Although we live in the age of technology, books are still essential. Recent research shows that there is a direct association between exposure to books in early childhood and literacy skills developed later on. Additionally, it is very important for bilingual children to experience books in both languages to increase their exposure to both languages.

Preschool and kindergarten are typically the years in which children learn "prereading" skills, such as phonics. Phonics lessons teach children the sounds that individual letters make. For example, you need to know the sounds that "c" "a" and "t" make to "decode" or read the printed word "cat." Rhyming, which we discussed in Step 4, is a great (and a fun) way to help kids learn letter sounds. Reading out loud and pointing to the words that you are reading is also an excellent way to help prime your child for learning to read.

How difficult should the books that I read to my child be?

As a rule of thumb, when you are reading to your child, aim for a language level that is just a little more advanced than the level your child is at. Reading specialists advise against choosing a book in which the language is too complex, because it can actually decrease comprehension and the joy of being read to. So, when you read to your child in a second language, you may need to choose a book that will be easier to understand than a book in your child's dominant language. This is just fine. Again, the focus should be on comprehension and enjoyment. Don't be concerned about teaching the maximum possible number of new words, or about choosing a book that is as challenging as one you might choose in, say, English.

Interactive books

Kids, especially those who have yet to learn to read, love storybooks that come with an accompanying cassette or CD that contains a "read-aloud" version of the story. As children listen to the story and follow along in the book, they feel like they are reading themselves and are very proud! These book-and-tape/CD combos can be especially helpful if you are not fluent in the language your child is learning as they give your child the opportunity to hear a fluent native speaker. And regardless of how well you speak the language, another advantage is that you can just pop in the tape or CD and be spared from having to read the same story over and over yourself!

Q&A: *My child is starting to learn to read by herself. Do I still have to read to her?*

Any trained children's librarian or literacy specialist will tell you to continue to read to your child at least until she has solid reading and reading comprehension skills, which is usually achieved somewhere toward the end of elementary school. Some experts now encourage parents to keep reading aloud to their children and discussing what they've read even beyond that, saying that it can help continue to strengthen a child's general language skills regardless of how well she reads. The advantage to continuing to read to your child even after she starts to read on her own is that it helps expand her vocabulary and comprehension of more complex language, which she may

11 "Tricks of the Trade" for Reading to Your Child
in Your Language

1. *Do not be concerned if you are not absolutely fluent in your second language.* Most children's books are simple enough for you to get by.

2. *Look for books that reflect your child's interests.* If your daughter loves ballet, pick up a book on ballerinas from your local library.

3. *At this stage don't worry too much if the book is in English.* Simply "read" the book in your language by translating as you go along.

4. *Try to choose books with pictures.* The pictures will help your child understand the story better and aid in learning new vocabulary, such as Little Red Riding Hood's *cape.*

5. *Talk to your child in your language about the story while reading it and after you have finished.* This will help you gauge how well he understands it. You can ask open-ended questions, such as "Would you have liked that if it happened to you?" or specifics about the story such as "Who was the story about?"

6. *If the book is written in your language and your child is old enough, encourage him to attempt to recognize and read some of the frequently used words.* It's fine to stop and point to the easy words so your child can read them out loud himself, but try not to break the rhythm of the story too much.

7. *Keep your goals achievable and simple.* One or two new vocabulary words per story time is fine. Then, the next time you read the book, add two more.

8. *Try pointing to pictures or explaining in your language before translating.* This keeps your child in your language and in the mode of trying to "figure out," which is an important bilingual skill.

9. *If you are reading a more complicated story, try giving a simplified version the first time.* (Base it on the pictures.) Once your child has a basic understanding of the plot, try reading straight from the text.

10. *Encourage your child to pull out a book that she wants you to read to her.* A child that enjoys being read to will look forward to learning to read.

11. *Above all, keep the experience fun.* A child who associates reading with pleasure, like snuggling up with mommy or daddy, is likely to become a life-long reader.

not be getting—or grasping—from the books she reads herself. Also, reading out loud to your child exposes her to a fluent reading style at a time when she is likely to be reading at a hesitant pace.

Early Elementary Grades: Time to Read!

The first question that many parents who want their child to learn to read in their language ask me is, "What is the best, most efficient way for my child to learn to read in two languages?" They want to know if their child should start off learning to read in English and then move toward reading in the other language, or learn to read in both languages simultaneously.

The truth is, it doesn't really matter. Either way can work just fine. But what does matter—a great deal—is the quality and comprehensiveness of the instruction. To learn to read well in two languages, a child must receive clear and simple instruction in the "reading rules" that apply to each language.

When I tell this to parents, I'm often asked, "If learning to read in my language is really about learning the rules, can't I just teach my child myself?" My answer is you can, but if you don't have the support of a tutor or a weekend school that can offer formal reading instruction as a "back up," I do advise using a home curricula, such as those discussed in Step 4. Why? Because for most of us, the reading rules in our language have become so instinctive that oftentimes we can't even remember all of them. Also, unless you're trained as a teacher, it's important to have some kind of support and structure so you can know how to teach the "rules" most effectively.

As we discussed earlier, it's pretty much inevitable that once your child reaches school age, her dominant language will be English. So don't be concerned if your child's reading level in your language is one or two grade levels below her reading level in English. As long as you and she keep at it, little by little she'll start to read more fluently in your language.

**6 Things You Can Do *Now* That Will Encourage Your Child to
Become a Life-Long Reader in Your Language**

1. *Make sure your child sees you reading in your language.* Believe it or not, this may be *the* most effective thing you can do inspire your child to read in your language. Marc told me, "I kept wondering where my Spanish Sunday paper was going and then I found it in my son Anthony's room!" If Marc had not had the Spanish paper in the house in the first place, and probably if Anthony had not seen his father reading it, he would not have picked it up himself. Research shows a direct relationship between a rich reading environment at home and higher reading skills in children, in any language.

2. *Keep in mind that reading in a second language is more tiring, so adjust your expectations accordingly.* The books your child reads in your language should be easier than the books he reads in English. Realize, too, that your child will probably not be able to read for as long in your language as he can in English. At first he may only "last" for a few minutes, and that's just fine.

3. *Help your child learn to recognize, at an automatic level, words that tend to come up multiple times in writing.* This can make reading less laborious and more fun. Oftentimes you can buy flashcards with the one hundred or two hundred most frequently used words in a language, but try not to use them in a "drill-like" and/or "test-like" way. For flashcards to be fun and effective, your child should know the vast majority of the words, and you should increase the number of cards slowly. Also, try to make a game out of it when you use them. For instance, some kids like to be timed and beat their record time. And of course kids love being awarded points for every one that's correct, and seeing how high they can run up the score.

4. *Consider putting labels on the items around your house that correspond to frequently used words.* For example, you could put a label with the word for "chair" in your language on the back of the chair and a label with the word for "door" on the door. Some parents might find these labels annoying, but the upside is that your child ends up seeing the word so many times that it is bound to sink in, without any conscious effort on your child's part. Another advantage to labels is that they

can reinforce comprehension in context. For example, if you say to your child in your language, "Can you please open the door for me?" your child looks right at the word for door as he opens it.

5. *Give your beginning reader an opportunity to show off her skills.* When you are reading to your child and a word comes up that you know that she knows stop so that she can say the word. This can be very empowering for kindergartners and first graders, especially.

6. *Share the reading.* Once your child has started reading in your language, take turns reading the pages of a book: you read one page, your child reads one page. This speeds up the flow and makes the story more exciting and accessible to your child, while also giving her a chance to practice reading.

Upper Elementary Grades: Read on!

When your child reaches the upper elementary grades, she will be speaking your language much more fluently. Her reading will be more fluent, too. Seeing the fruits of your and your child's labors makes this an exciting time. But do keep in mind that at this point, your child will be able to read much more easily in English than in your language, so to keep her reading in your language, it is going to be important to identify books and materials in your language that she *wants* to read.

Meeting at-home reading requirements

It's common for children in the upper elementary school grades (usually third grade and higher) to be required to read approximately 30 minutes per day at home. I am often asked by parents if they can split the 30 minutes between both languages. This is a tough question to answer, and here's why: One of the reasons schools require daily reading at home is to help advance children's reading ability and reading comprehension skills—in English. And one of the reasons they want to do this is to help kids perform better in class and on standardized tests, which are conducted in English. As a parent you probably are already well aware of the tremendous pressure that schools, teachers, parents, and students face regarding standardized test performance.

On the other hand, if your child reads every day in your language, even for just ten minutes, it will certainly increase his reading and speaking proficiency in *your* language. So, rather than tell parents whether they should or shouldn't break up the time, I explain the advantages to each way, and tell them it is up to them to decide. One solution would be to read for 30 minutes a day in English *and* 10 minutes in your language. But I know that for some kids half the work is getting the book out and starting to read. If that's the case in your house, it might make more sense for your child to read for 30 minutes in your language instead of English one day during the school week. And try to fit in some more reading time in your language over the weekend, too.

Bilingual books can make reading fun

Parents often ask me about bilingual books, in which the text is written both in a foreign language and in English. People often think that bilingual books are "just for the little ones" and are only available in picture-book format. However, they can be found at all levels, including advanced literature. These books can be more expensive than books written in a single language, but they can be a terrific option, especially if your child is not quite fluent enough to read a book written solely in your language. Bilingual books can make a second language attainable and, as a result, the reading experience much more enjoyable. For many parents that alone makes the extra cost worth it, because if a child finds reading unpleasant, he won't do it at all.

Keep your reading material radar always on

Once your child is able to read more complex material, be on the look-out for books, magazine or newspaper articles, or really just about anything written in your language that you think he might enjoy reading. You might say, "Did you know that France made it to the Rugby World Cup semifinals? I saved this newspaper article about it. I thought you might be interested." (See Step 4, and the Resource List at the end of the book for ideas that can help you maximize written language input.)

The Write Stuff

Writing in a second language is like the "final frontier"—the fourth language skill, after listening, speaking, and reading. But it's a frontier well worth exploring. For some parents, though, the mere thought of writing in a second language is enough to make *them* cringe, as they think back to their school years and remember, perhaps, the whole writing experience as being quite tiresome. But I hope to show you here that your children do not need to learn to write in your language in the same rigid way that you did. And while it's true that some children are naturally more creative than others, I believe that there is a writer in everyone, and everyone can benefit from—and experience joy and pride in—expressing themselves through written language. But learning to write in your language is not just a nice creative exercise for your child. It can help him become much more proficient in your language. Here's how:

1. **Writing helps to reinforce vocabulary.** When a child writes a sentence, he must use words in context, which is a much better way of learning and reinforcing vocabulary than simply memorizing lists of words and their definitions. Encourage your child to use a *word bank*

(a short list of new words and their meanings) when he writes. Incorporating these words into his writing task will make it easier for him to create the text and will help him better learn and remember the words.

2. **Writing helps us learn and practice grammar skills.** Writing is a great medium to learn and then consolidate grammar skills, including correct spelling, punctuation, and usage and structure of verbs. But don't expect your child to start out writing entire sentences from scratch with perfect spelling and grammar. Most children who learn to write in a school setting will probably fill out practice worksheets. These writing worksheets help consolidate skills they are learning. They have evolved a lot from the days when we were at school, and the educators that develop these tools design them to be as fun as possible while teaching vocabulary and grammar skills, such as writing in the verb in the correct tense.

3. **Writing helps to develop a deeper, more nuanced understanding of the language.** For example, in English it is only by reading and writing that one understands that there is a difference between "there" and "their." From only listening and speaking it would be difficult, if not impossible, to know that the two words have different spellings. Writing, too, helps cement knowledge of the many idioms, or distinct figures of speech, that crop up in every language, and to remember that in Italian, for example, you *hai perso,* or "lost," the bus, while in English, you "missed" it.

4. **Writing helps develop higher language skills.** Compared to spoken language, which is fluent and casual, written language requires more precise word choices and more complex and carefully structured sentences. In the same way that reading a language requires more complex thinking in that language and higher level language skills, so does writing down thoughts.

5. **Writing helps to improve spoken language skills.** Written language has a "fixed" and unmoving nature. The beauty of this is that if a child makes a mistake, such as putting words in an incorrect order, he can literally see the difference between his usage and the correct one. And this learning will carry over into his spoken language. So as your child progresses with his writing, you will notice that his spoken language will become more accurate, too.

Q&A: *Should I correct my child's writing?*

There is some controversy as to how much adults should correct children's writing out of concern that it will discourage children from expressing themselves and attempting to write longer and more complex sentences. But most educators agree that correction can be very valuable as long as it's done in a nonthreatening way. In other words, please don't just mark up your child's work with a red pencil and hand it back to him! It's important not to simply point out mistakes, but to explain why and how they need to be changed. Having that conversation will help your child understand and remember the information the next time he sits down to write. And always find something to praise about your child's work and express that before telling your child what he did wrong. You might say, "You followed the rule well here, but this particular word just happens to be an exception and is written like this . . ." . Finally, try to limit your corrections to spelling, grammar, and punctuation, and even if you are working on structure, try to avoid rewriting your child's thoughts and ideas.

The 6 Skill Levels of Writing in a Second Language

As with learning to understand, speak, and read in a second language, children learn best how to write in a second language through fun activities geared to their skill level. Here's a guide:

Skill Level 1: Prewriting

At its most basic, writing is expressing thoughts and ideas by putting symbols on paper. You can help your young child get used to this concept by encouraging her to draw. Through drawing, preschoolers and children in younger grades learn that there's another way besides speaking to express their thoughts and ideas *and* that what they put down on paper has meaning. Even the youngest child has an inkling that her pictures stand for something.

Drawing is also a great way to illustrate (quite literally) the link between thoughts and ideas and written language. For example, the next time you read a story with your child, you might ask her to draw a character from the story. If she draws, say, an "angry lion," then you can write "angry lion" in your language underneath her picture. These first attempts toward writing represent a growing awareness of the existence of written language and an understanding that it is a form of expression. As time goes on, encourage your child to try to copy or to write captions for her picture herself. Ask her in your language, "So what do you want to write under your picture?" Conversing in your language will prompt her to speak and think in your language, and avoid translating from English.

Skill Level 2: Starting to Write Words

As your child attempts to write his first words in your language, you will notice that he relies on what he had learned so far about writing in his dominant language. At this skill level he will use the same phonetic rules from, say, English, to write in your language. As a result, some of the words might look strange. Not to worry, this is a normal stage of development. In fact you probably witnessed the same thing when your child first started writing in English. For example, he might have written "i no hu u r" instead of "I know who you are."

144

Many educators stress that at this early stage, especially, it is more important to encourage the act of writing than it is to focus too intently on how the words are written. Simply praise your child for his effort and gently correct him by saying, "That's a great try! But that word is a little tricky. It's actually written like this. . . ."

Keep in mind, too, that your child wasn't born knowing the particulars of writing in English. He learned them through teaching and practice. He will learn the particulars of writing in your language in the same way.

Continue (and this advice really goes for all levels) to speak in your language to your child about her work in your language. It's important to do this because it can help your child avoid composing sentences in English first and then translating them into your language, which can lead to some very odd sentences. It also gives you the opportunity to help her learn, and learn how to write, new words in your language.

Skill Level 3: Starting to Write Sentences

In the same way that your child might have first turned to the English phonetic rules he is familiar with when writing words in your language, when it comes writing sentences in your language, he may also first turn to his knowledge of constructing sentences in English. This can lead once again to the incorrect word order in your language. And again, that's why from the beginning, it's so important to encourage your child to think in your language when he writes in your language.

Recognize that at this early writing stage your child will gravitate to writing about personally significant topics. He'll write frequently used phrases and expressions, such as "Hello, my name is Josh. What is your name?" He might also write about an event that took place: "I went to a super birthday party," or "I cooked a cake with Auntie. We put it in the oven and forgot it. It burned." Encourage this, as it helps to solidify in your child's mind that writing is an expression of one's thoughts and ideas.

Also, just because your child can now write, don't dismiss drawing. As I said above, drawings are inner pictures, or symbols, of what a child wants to say. Therefore, drawing a picture can help the writing process because it helps kids become aware of and develop their thoughts and ideas, a necessary step before you can write them down. (To put it another way, drawing can help overcome "writer's block.") Some teachers have found drawing to be such an effective way to bring ideas and thoughts to the surface that they encourage students to start off by drawing before writing, or to write and draw together.

Skill Level 4: Writing Short Paragraphs (Beginner's Level)

At this level kids are fledging writers who are just beginning to test their "writing wings." So try to avoid doing anything to discourage them, such as assigning them a daunting topic to write about! Instead, encourage your child to write about her own experiences and things she is familiar with, such as her favorite TV show or what she wants to do on her birthday. At this age kids are full of imagination and curiosity so you might encourage your child to write an alternative ending to a popular story, such as *Goldilocks and the Three Bears.* What would have happened if Goldilocks had knocked at the door and the bears were home?

This skill level also presents the perfect opportunity to reinforce and learn new vocabulary. Teachers will often give students at this level word banks to use when writing. For example, in a paragraph imagining an alternative ending to *The Three Bears,* children could be given the words *oatmeal, chair,* and *bed* in their language. Again, giving beginning writers a word bank to draw from when they write helps with the flow of the writing and also helps them learn and remember the specific words and their spelling.

Also, at this level, it's fine, even advisable, to help your child construct a paragraph. The operative word, however, is "help." Resist writing the paragraph yourself. Instead, ask your child a series of "W" questions to get his ideas flowing: *Who* are you going to write about? *Where* does the story take place? *What* is the character going to do?

Finally, be aware that at this level in particular there is a tendency for children to compose in their minds what they want to say in English and then translate it into their second language as they write it down. This can happen quite automatically because for all of us thinking is easier and more elaborate in our dominant language. But as I mentioned earlier, this can lead to very odd sentences, and it is not a habit you want your child to develop. It's a good idea from the start to remind children *not* to translate and to reassure them that it is fine to write shorter and more simple sentences than they would write in English. Also, if at all possible, converse in your language while your child is writing in your language.

Skill Level 5: Intermediate Level

As your child becomes more used to and adept at writing in your language, you'll find he writes more quickly. While basic grammar or spelling difficulties tend to lessen, at this stage your child is writing longer sentences that often require using more complex grammar, such as different tenses, positive/negative statements, and adjectives and adverbs, all of which may result in mistakes. Assure your child that this is okay. Let him know that it is more important that he take the risk of writing more complex and longer sentences than it is that he write perfectly. Reassure him that you or his teacher will go over the work and help him correct any mistakes later. Emphasize the importance of writing more than one draft, and reading over and correcting each draft to produce the next. Even though this might seem tedious, children are proud once the final and best draft is completed.

Skill Level 6: Advanced Level

A youngster who reaches an advanced level of writing in a second language makes few grammar and spelling mistakes and is able to call upon a rich vocabulary, which he has gained in part from extensive reading in the second language. He is also able to research a topic in the second language and then summarize and synthesize the information and offer his own observations and conclusions in that language.

If this skill level seems like a long way off for your child, just keep in mind the Japanese proverb, "A journey of a thousand miles begins with a single step." Advanced writing skills begin with drawing pictures and writing words underneath them.

Writing in a Second Language: What to Expect

Children usually write in their second language one or two levels below their oral skills in that language, as well as one or two levels below their writing skills in their dominant language. As a result, for most kids, writing in the second language is going to be slower and require more effort than it does in their dominant language.

Let your child know that "it's okay if you write slowly, because all kids write more slowly in their other language." Not surprisingly, one researcher found that it took college students who were learning English as a second language three times longer to write a page in English than it took students who were English dominant. Also let kids know that it is fine if they make mistakes. Tell them that for now, it is inevitable that they are going to make more mistakes in their second language than they do in their dominant language because they are less proficient in that language and they practice it less.

10 Ways To Encourage Your Child to Write in Your Language

1. *Encourage your child to read in your language.* The 2007 Nobel Prize in literature was awarded to Doris Lessing, a writer who never finished high school, but taught herself through voracious reading. Reading helps students learn vocabulary and develop sensitivity to written language, including how sentences are structured and where to put the punctuation. It also helps children develop a relationship with written work and become familiar with the hallmarks of good writing, such as what elements make a good story, and incorporate that knowledge into their own writing.

2. *Encourage your child to think in your language when writing and not to translate from English.* Your child might have the tendency to think in her dominant language and then translate it into her second language as she is writing. You want to discourage this as it leads to incorrect sentence structure and awkward sentences in general. Instead, encourage her to write in your language and simply to write shorter, simpler sentences.

3. *Encourage your child to use a "word bank" while writing because a word bank will assist his writing.* A word bank is especially helpful when your child has not yet mastered a vast array of words. It can help prevent her from becoming discouraged when she can't "find" a word and it can help consolidate the learning of new ones. It also can make the writing process go faster.

4. *Encourage your child to write about what he's reading or learning.* You want to encourage your child to write about topics that are relevant to his life, including what he is reading or learning in school, for two reasons: one, because they're likely to be more interesting to him, and two, because the task makes sense to him—to a young child, writing about an abstract topic does not make sense.

5. *Encourage your child to write about what is interesting to him.* If at all possible, a child should not be assigned a particular topic to write about until he is quite far along in his spoken and written language proficiency. Again, the focus should

Continued

149

be on getting your child to write, and he's much more likely to be motivated to do so if he can write about whatever *he* wants. If this is a problem at your child's second language school (especially if your child is at the elementary school level), talk with the second language teacher and say, "My son is having trouble with writing a poem, but he told me that he would willingly write a paragraph on airplanes. Is this okay?"

6. *Encourage your child to tell you a story.* As your child tells the story, write it down on a piece of paper or type it on the computer. This breaks down the writing process (your child comes up with the sentences, you do the writing), and gives your child the immediate feeling of success. After all, he did just "write" a story! This can be especially fruitful in a second language, where it's even more of a challenge to actually express thoughts on paper. Parents who try this activity for fun often tell me, "I never knew that my son (or daughter) could speak so well, and his creativity blew me away."

7. *Encourage your child to "just write."* It can be hard enough to start writing in one's dominant language, but as I said above, it's even more challenging in a second language. So it's even more important to encourage children to just start writing without stopping to judge what they're writing. Tell your child, "Just write, and we will have a look later."

8. *Encourage your child to write in your language by doing so yourself.* When you leave notes for your child, make shopping lists, and keep track of family members' schedules make an effort to write in your language. This way you create an even richer second language environment, and one in which your child sees that writing in the second language is natural.

9. *Encourage your child to have a pen pal.* If you had a pen pal when you were a child, you communicated via "snail mail," and letters from overseas took weeks to arrive. Your child can connect instantly with another child halfway around the world via e-mail. Friends and relatives who speak your language can be e-mail (or snail mail) correspondents, too. But as always with children and the Internet, keep in mind safety and privacy guidelines. (For more on these guidelines visit the American Academy of Pediatrics official web site on Internet safety at www.safetynet.aap.org).

10. *Encourage your child to keep a daily journal.* A journal is a great way to ensure that writing becomes a daily habit, and kids usually love it. "Whenever something comes up during the day, both my kids will shout 'That's going in my diary!,' " says Lisa, the mom of two girls, ages 7 and 9. "They never leave home with their diary notepads. They seem like reporters to me!" I also like to encourage children to use their journals as a way of expressing themselves beyond recording the day's events. Journals can include collages, drawings, photos, stickers, and postcards. This way a child feels, "I created this, it is unique and mine." It is in effect his first book, and he has every right to feel proud of it.

Q&A: *Help! My son is learning to write in German but his teacher at school told me that she has noticed some unusual mistakes in English. What should I do?*

As we discussed, spelling and grammar rules are probably going to be different in your language than they are in English. Some words, like *chi* in Italian and "key" in English, to use the example I gave earlier, sound similar but are spelled differently and have different meanings. Grammar rules also vary from language to language. In German, for example, all nouns start with a capital letter, while in English only proper nouns do. But in my experience, any mixing of rules is usually temporary and, given time, children learning two languages consolidate the rules in each language and no longer mix them up. But it is very important for parents not to panic during this "sorting out" period and not to abandon their long-term goal of biliteracy. It may be helpful to explain to your child's teacher, who most likely has been trained to teach monolingual children, that your child is in the process of learning not one, but two sets of spelling and grammar rules and that he just needs time to master them both. This way, the teacher will not be baffled when she sees a few extra capital letters pop up!

Communication with the teacher is key for your child's sake too. As I've said before, it's important that a child learning two languages feel proud of that fact, and you don't want your child to view his second language as a drag on his ability to do well in school. In my experience, discussion and creativity on the part of parent and teacher usually lead to solutions that reinforce to the child that he is progressing just fine. For instance, it might be possible for the teacher to write something on a your child's paper such as "Great job, Peter. I saw some German capitals in there. Remember in English only names have capitals. I am sure that you will soon figure out how this works—in English and in German!"

7

Adapting to School: The Bilingual Child Goes to School

Children, whether they are being raised monolingual or bilingual, are increasingly exposed to other languages and other cultures as early as preschool, thanks in large part to a seemingly unlikely source: television. But, I must quickly add, the credit doesn't go to the vast majority of shows on TV, but rather to the quality children's programs. *Sesame Street,* which hit the airwaves in 1969, has long been dedicated to representing different languages and cultures, but more recently it has been joined by *Maya and Miguel* and the popular *Dora the Explorer,* which teaches Spanish expressions, as well *Madeline,* who has made the leap from the pages of the classic children's books to the small screen where she greets viewers by saying, "*Bonjour, mes amis.*" Even Quetzal, the wise dragon teacher on *Dragon Tales,* a PBS show aimed at preschoolers, is bilingual!

The good news is that in a world drawn ever closer by globalization and technology, the ability to speak as well as read and write in a second language is now regarded as more valuable and more necessary than ever by both bilingual parents *and* monolingual English-speaking parents. The not-so-good news is that private bilingual schools are financially out of reach for most families and the opportunity to receive a true bilingual education in the public school system has yet to catch up with the demand. The truth is that much of the time "bilingual education" in public schools is another name for teaching English to students who have just immigrated to the United States, so that they can be assimilated as quickly as possible into a mainstream English-only classroom. In other words, there's very little bilingual about it.

The news is not all bleak, however. The desire of parents to raise their children bilingual is becoming increasingly recognized, and some public school systems have already implemented—and, with pressure from parents like you and me, more may be coaxed into implementing—programs that support long-term goals for bilingualism and biliteracy.

In this seventh and final Step, I will discuss the academic considerations that accompany raising a bilingual child. I've broken the discussion down into two parts:

Part One: Bilingual education programs: Where we've been, where we're at, and where we're going In this section, I will take a brief look at the history of public bilingual education in the United States, what kind of programs are typically offered now, and hopefully, what kind of programs we will see more of in the future. This knowledge will help you better assess and utilize (or steer clear of, as the case may be!) the bilingual and foreign language learning opportunities that your public school system offers.

Part Two: Results may vary: How to handle special situations that can affect your child's bilingual academic progress In this section, I will offer guidance for dealing with special situations such as giftedness, developmental delays, and difficulty with reading and writing.

Part One: Public Bilingual Education Programs: Where We've Been, Where We're at, and Where We're Going

The public school systems in the United States offer an array of bilingual education programs, which sounds like great news for parents who are raising their children bilingual, until, as I mentioned earlier in this Step, you realize that the main goal of most of these programs is to provide intense English instruction to children who have little or no proficiency in English. Sadly then, despite their name, the majority, although not all, of bilingual programs don't promote true bilingualism (in fact, they promote just the opposite). However, some school districts *do* offer programs that support bilingual and biliteracy goals, and there is increasing recognition of their value and their popularity, which hopefully will mean that their number, and the number of languages they're offered in, will grow in the coming years.

A Short History of Public Bilingual Education in the United States

Most people are unaware that there is precedent in the United States for teaching classes in public schools in a language other than English. For example, during the early 1900s, classes at a large concentration of public elementary schools in the Midwest were taught in German.

In 1963 the Cuban immigrant community in Dade County, Florida, developed the first truly bilingual public schools in the United States. They taught both Spanish-speaking children and English-speaking children in the community how to read and write in both Spanish and English.

Throughout much of the rest of the United States however, the children of immigrants were "submerged" into classes that were taught in English and were, in essence, told to "sink or swim." Unfortunately, but not surprisingly, most of these children "sank" and failed academically. Immigrants and their supporters hoped that a series of acts passed by the U.S. Congress in the 1960s, including the Civil Rights Act of 1964, the Elementary and Secondary Education Act of 1965, and the Bilinguals Act of 1968, which acknowledged that children who cannot speak English have special education needs that must be addressed, would help reverse this dismal trend. But the situation didn't change significantly until 1974, when the U.S. Supreme Court heard the case, *Lau vs. Nichols.*

The Lau case was brought before the court on behalf of a group of non-English-speaking Chinese-American students in San Francisco, who were immersed in classrooms where all of the instruction was given in English. The Court ruled that placing students in a classroom in which the instruction is given in a language that they don't understand deprives them of an equal opportunity to receive an education, and it mandated that public schools offer non-English-speaking students access to the same curriculum as English-speaking students.

However, the Supreme Court justices did not specify *how* schools should do this, and more than 30 years after the Lau decision, there is still considerable political and educational debate about what is the most effective way to do it. While this dilemma may not affect you directly, understanding the different approaches that school systems take can give you a better understanding of what constitutes bilingual education in the public school system today.

Transitional Bilingual Programs

Most school systems have opted to fulfill the Lau mandate by focusing on teaching English to non-English-speaking students, rather than teaching them the curriculum in their native language. Indeed, 28 percent of non-English-speaking elementary-school students do not receive *any* instruction in their native language, and of those who do, approximately one-third still receive 75 percent of their curriculum instruction in English. (Another third receives 40 to 75 percent of their instruction in English, and the final third receive 40 percent or less of their instruction in English.) At the middle and high school level, students receive even less instruction in their native language.

Although there are no easy solutions, particularly in classrooms where several different languages are represented, it is unfortunate that students are not able to receive more instruction in their native languages because research shows that when they do, they not only have a better understanding of the subject matter being taught, but they also develop a better understanding of English! That may sound odd, but remember, many language skills are "transferable" from one language to another. So, given that, it's not so surprising that strong native language skills help to strengthen English language skills.

For better or worse (and sadly, sometimes it's for the worse), the emphasis in transitional bilingual programs is on teaching students a minimum of English as quickly as possible and then transitioning them into regular classrooms. Lack of guidelines for these programs remains an on-going issue, as it can be unclear how much help teachers are required to give children to support their learning of other subjects while they are learning English and what criteria should be used to determine when a student is proficient enough in English to be able to succeed in a regular classroom. After a certain point, though, it may not matter, as these programs frequently have a time limit (usually around five years) at which point the students are mainstreamed into regular classrooms regardless of whether they are truly proficient enough in English to learn academic subjects that are taught in English. The problem with this, of course, is that many of these students do not have sufficient English language skills to understand what is being said in the classroom. So they then spend their time simply trying to figure out what the teacher is saying, rather than learning the subject that is being taught.

ESL, or English as a Second Language, Programs

This approach may be familiar to you as it is used in many school systems. Students split their time between the regular classroom and the ESL classroom, where their sole goal is to learn English. The amount of hours spent in the ESL classroom can vary, as can the level of skills of the students—even in one instruction group. The upside is that teachers are usually specially trained to teach English to English language learners and to make an effort to be sensitive to students' native cultures. But ESL programs make no attempt to provide ongoing support for learning in students' native language or to help students keep and develop skills in their language.

Two-Way, or Dual, Immersion Programs

Unlike transitional programs, two-way or dual, immersion programs do *not* aim for rapid assimilation into the regular classroom, but instead provide equal instruction in two languages for the long term. Another important difference is that dual immersion programs are not just for children whose native language is not English. Oftentimes, half of the students participating in these programs are monolingual English-speaking children, allowing for a cultural exchange.

These programs are based on the following understanding:

- Knowledge and skills are transferable from one language to another.
- Strengthening native language skills helps strengthen English language skills and vice versa.
- Reaching a high proficiency level in a second language takes years. There is a big difference in the language skills necessary to make everyday conversation and the language skills necessary to succeed in an academic setting.

- A child has the right to maintain his native language while acquiring solid English language proficiency, and his language and culture are as valuable as English and American culture.

Another advantage to dual immersion programs is that children for whom English is a second language get the opportunity to learn to read and write in their native language, and as a result, gain access to higher language and higher cognitive skills. This is an extremely important intellectual boost and one that children who enter school with limited English language skills and who are solely exposed to reading in English can miss out on developing.

Follow-up reports on these programs have been very positive. Although most dual immersion programs only cover the elementary years, the "alumni" of one Spanish/English program, interviewed when they were in high school, reported that they still spoke Spanish and had a positive attitude towards school and college.

Needless to say then, dual immersion programs can be a great opportunity for parents who are raising their children bilingual. A problem, though, besides the fact that they're mostly at the elementary level, is that only a few hundred elementary schools in the entire country currently offer dual immersion programs and the vast majority of them pair up the same language with English: Spanish. In 2006, there were a total of 338 dual immersion programs in public elementary schools in the United States. Of these, 316 were Spanish/English, according to Center for Applied Linguistics.

But that's the "cup-half-empty" view. The "cup-half-full" view is that hundreds of these programs already do exist and have a proven track record of developing strong skills in two languages and positive feelings toward two cultures. As a parent, you can point to these programs and push your own school district to implement them and to increase the number of languages in which they're offered. It may not feel like it, but as a parent, especially if you band together with other parents, you have a lot of clout with school officials. For starters, you along with all the other voters in your school district elect the school board. Even if your school system has traditionally offered only French and Spanish, you can still speak up and work to try to change or expand the languages taught in your individual school.

For example, one school principal told me that he always asks parents to write comments and suggestions on the form in which they indicate whether they want their child to take Spanish or French. "Direct, written feedback from parents makes it much easier for me to go to the head of the foreign language department and make the case that I want to trade one Spanish teacher for a teacher of another foreign language," he told me.

5 Things You Need to Know about Foreign Language Study in U.S. Public Schools

1. Know what bilingual education programs your school system offers.

I recommend that all parents who are raising their children bilingual become familiar with the bilingual educational opportunities that are available in their public school system. One of the simplest ways to do this can be to get in touch with your school system's foreign language department, sometimes called world languages department, or the school system's English as a Second Language (ESL) program director. Also, while an ESL program is probably not the type of program that you are looking for, most likely the director is aware of the different bilingual opportunities in your school system and can explain them to you.

If there is a two-way immersion program offered in your language, call the school immediately and arrange a visit! I tell parents that visiting a prospective school and observing classes is one of the most important things they can do. Take a look around and ask questions. Think about whether the school's approach and atmosphere would be a good "fit" for your child.

2. Know that true bilingual programs are relatively rare and extremely popular.

Start your research early and do not hesitate to put your child's name down on the waiting list as early as the school or program will take it. Realize that established public bilingual programs and/or schools are so popular that placement is usually determined by lottery or waiting list, and sometimes both! At the Bilingual Public Charter School in Washington, D.C., which offers bilingual instruction in Spanish and English, there's a waiting list *and* a lottery system to get in. (Places in good, reasonably priced bilingual programs go fast, too. There is a waiting list of students eager to enter Boston's German Saturday school, Deutsche Sonnabendschüle.) In most cases, if you wait till it's time to enroll your child in kindergarten it will be too late to grab a spot, although many schools will guarantee admission to younger siblings of kids who are already in the program.

Some parents will go the extra mile (literally) to secure their child a spot in a public bilingual school. Madeleine told me, "Soon after Dylan was born we were looking to move out of our apartment into a house. I checked all the school districts in the areas where we could see ourselves living, and I found a one that had a Spanish/English magnet school. So we moved there! Some of our friends and relatives thought we were crazy to move to a town just because of a school, especially when our son was only a few months old. But raising Dylan bilingual is a priority for us, and we thought that it was a good sign that the town supported such a school."

3. Know that in most school districts, rigorous foreign language study happens at the high school level.

While children can sometimes take a foreign language in middle school, most "serious" foreign language instruction, with the goal of learning to speak and read and write in the language, is still relegated to high school. As I mentioned in Step 4, the percentage of elementary schools offering foreign language instruction is up, but 41 percent of elementary schools that offer instruction do so via FLEX programs. FLEX stands for "Foreign Language Exploratory" or "Foreign Language Experience" program. Be aware that the goal of most of these programs is to expose monolingual students to an array of foreign languages and other cultures in general. While that's a worthy goal in and of itself, don't expect that these programs will provide the structure that's necessary to achieve bilingualism and biliteracy.

4. Know that language choice is often limited.

The array of foreign languages offered in public middle and high schools is increasing, but Spanish and French continue to be the most common. But the languages offered can change over the years, so it's worth talking to the head of the foreign language department at your child's middle school or high school (or if your child is in the upper elementary school grades, what will be her middle or high school). You can find out if any additional languages may be offered in the near future and also make your preferences known. You can also investigate if your school system offers your language at a middle or high school other than the school that your child attends or is slated to attend. If your language does happen to be offered at another school, you could consider requesting a transfer.

5. Know that "sequencing" is probably going to be an issue for your bilingual child.

Most public school foreign language programs, whether in elementary, middle, or high school, assume that children have no prior knowledge of the language and place *all* students in a Level 1 class accordingly. So if your child has been speaking the language for years and may be reading and writing in the language as well, being placed in a Level 1 class is obviously not going to contribute to his second language proficiency. It may even detract from it because he'll be bored and may lose his motivation to progress in it even in other venues, such as at home or in a weekend language school.

On the other hand, kids, particularly when they're in middle school, desperately want to fit in and might feel angst at being "different" from their peers. You may then want to consider signing your child up for another language other than your own, which allows your child to be with his classmates while avoiding exposure (potentially over and over again) to instruction in your language that is far too basic for him. Or, if your child is just starting middle school or high school and doesn't mind being in a class with older students, another option is to explain to the head of the foreign language department that your child has already achieved proficiency in the language and ask that he be placed in an advanced class that matches his skill level.

Part Two: Results May Vary: How to Handle Special Situations That Can Affect Your Child's Bilingual Academic Progress

If you have more than one child, or if you have siblings yourself, you know how children born to the same parents can be different from one another, despite being raised more or less the same. Each child's individuality shows itself when it comes to bilingualism, too. For example, you might find that your first child teaches himself to read in your language, while his younger sister mixes English words into her Russian for years. You're raising both of them more or less the same, so why the difference? Their temperaments, their interest in learning a second language and their aptitude for learning languages, for starters.

As a developmental and behavioral pediatrician I frequently find myself gently reminding the parents of *all* my patients (not just those who are being raised bilingual) to try to honor their children's individuality and talents and not to constantly compare siblings with each other. But that advice must truly be taken to heart when raising your children bilingual. You may start with the same bilingual plan for all your children, but you may need to adapt it for each child, depending on how he progresses.

The Talented Child

I often counsel parents who have what *sounds* like an enviable task, although in reality it is a considerable challenge: helping a talented child adapt to what is often for the child, an uninteresting school environment. These parents often go to great lengths to find intellectually stimulating programs and activities for their kids ranging from chess teams to science camps. But I like to tell these parents that foreign-language learning is one of the most mentally challenging activities they will find for their child because it requires the brain to constantly "figure out" what another person (or a book or written material) is trying to say. And because there are an inexhaustible number of conversations to be had and a countless number of books to read, the challenge is never ending. (There is also always another language to be learned, too!)

In addition, as we've discussed, language learning can be easily individualized—which is just what the doctor ordered for a talented child who often spends time at school waiting for some interesting information to come along. When it comes to language learning, your talented child doesn't have to wait for anyone else to catch up; she can simply move from learning to speak to learning to read and write in the language, and from there, move on to speaking with greater and greater fluency, reading more and more complex books, and writing more and more complex and longer paragraphs. While most children's ability to read in a second language is usually below their ability to read in their dominant language, a talented child might progress much faster and even close that gap. While it is unusual to be completely balanced in two languages, some children do reach a reading level in their second language that is similar to their level in English. I have seen this happen a number of times, and kids relate that while they might read a bit more slowly in their second language, they enjoy the extra challenge and are very proud of their accomplishment. Apparently, there is nothing like reading Harry Potter in Czech!

Linguistic Talent

There are also many children who receive adequate stimulation and challenge in the classroom when it comes to the usual curriculum subjects, but who possess a special aptitude for learning languages. Parents of these children will often comment on how their child started speaking early and has developed a rich vocabulary that surpasses that of his peers. For these children, it makes sense to introduce a second language early on, as it will tap into the same skill areas. Children who have special talent for languages often have the potential to attain near native-like fluency in speaking, reading and writing in a foreign language, which is exciting.

But don't forget that even in gifted children (linguistically and otherwise), talent alone is not enough. Like anyone else who attempts to learn a second language, these children must also have the inner motivation to learn that language.

The Child with Developmental Delay

While it's certainly no cause for worry (or frustration) if, say, your younger son displays merely an average ability to play baseball while his older brother is a star player, you *do* want to pay attention to whether each of your children is generally meeting the well-established developmental milestones and to seek help if they're not.

One giant developmental milestone of course is starting to talk. People often say that bilingual children start to speak later, yet as I mentioned in both Steps 1 and 2 research shows that bilingual children usually start speaking around the same time as monolingual children. If you are raising your child bilingual and you have concerns that he might be starting to talk later or is developing any other skill more slowly than other children, it is very unlikely that it has to do with bilingualism.

In my practice, I do not hesitate to refer a "late talker," monolingual or bilingual, to a specialist, called a speech and language therapist, for an evaluation, and here's why: Approximately 25 to 60 percent of monolingual "late talkers" continue to have language delays as preschoolers. Although receiving speech and language therapy does not automatically guarantee that these children will catch up with their same-age peers, increased and specific stimulation on the young, plastic brain can increase progress, so it is eminently worthwhile. In addition, children with early language delays may later show difficulties with phonological awareness. As we discussed in Step 6, phonological awareness is the foundation of learning to read, so if your child exhibits some delay in starting to talk and combine words into sentences you really do not want to leave things to chance, which is why I strongly advise consulting a speech and language therapist.

On the other hand, as we discussed in Steps 1 and 2, bilingual preschoolers *do* sometimes experience a "language lag." Unlike a child with language delay, a child with a language lag initially lags behind his same-age peers, but eventually catches up to them. But it's important to note that bilingual children who experience a language lag typically lag behind in being able to *express* themselves only, as opposed to a more general type of language delay where a child has difficulty expressing himself *and* understanding others. While bilingual children who experience language lags most likely will fully catch up without any "outside help," there is no way to know in advance. So if you're at all concerned about the pace of your child's language development, discuss your concerns with your child's pediatrician. And because it's much better to be safe than sorry, have your child evaluated and monitored, ideally by a speech and language therapist who has experience in assessing bilingual children.

If my child is a late-talker, will he be better off if I abandon my bilingual goals for him altogether?

No—although you would not always have been given that answer. The thinking used to be that if bilingual parents of a child with speech and language delay would just stop trying to teach him his heritage language and focus instead on teaching him English, it would aid his language development. However, fortunately, in recent years, research has clearly shown that this is simply not true. In the vast majority of the cases (and as I've said over and over again in this book), language skills are transferable. Moreover, the thing that a child with speech and language delay needs most of all is communication, which he won't get if he is cut off from conversations in the home.

Okay, so I can continue to raise my child bilingual. But what does this mean on a practical basis?

It means you're going to need to revisit your bilingual goals, plan, and:

1. **Readjust your expectations.** For instance, your child might be less fluent than her siblings and might not get to the same reading level.
2. **Readjust the time frame that it will take to reach each milestone.** A child with speech and language delay might require more repetitions of a word before she "picks it up."
3. **Increase consistency.** If communication and comprehension are more challenging for your child, you want to make an extra effort to give her as many opportunities as possible to be exposed to your language and to be as clear as possible when you are speaking with her. Also, in this situation it's even more

imperative that you try not to mix languages when talking with your child.

The Child Who Has Difficulty with Reading and Writing

Just to reiterate what I said in Step 6, generally, if a child is able to decode words in one language, he will be able decode them in the other. And if a child is having difficulty decoding in one language, then chances are that he will also have difficulty decoding in the other. The reason for this is that even though every language has its own specific rules, decoding is a general skill that can be applied to all languages. If your child has difficulty learning to read in English at school, hopefully she will be evaluated by a reading specialist at the school. (If this is not done, then you should push for it to be done.) The specialist may diagnose dyslexia, a learning disability that is neurological in nature and that makes it difficult to decode the sounds letters make, and to read and spell accurately and fluently. But it's important to note that while dyslexia is a learning disability, it has nothing to do with innate intelligence. In fact, many people with dyslexia have above average intelligence or are gifted.

So if my child has difficulty reading, what does it mean on a practical basis as far as bilingualism?

- You may need to readjust your bilingual goals and plan (especially if you were planning on teaching your child to read and write in your language). But as with a child with language delay, you don't have to abandon bilingualism completely.
- These adjustments mean that you may have to *deemphasize* or delay *temporarily* teaching your child to read in your language, and make developing his reading skills in English a priority. This is because reading in English is absolutely essential to his success at school. But don't think that all hope is lost for your

child reading in your language. Remember, a solid foundation of reading skills in one language (in this case English) can later enable reading skills in the second language.

- There's another reason not to put too much emphasis on reading and writing in your language: You want your child to continue to identify positively with your language, and if reading and writing is a struggle, and he's made to do it in your language, there's a good chance he'll feel negatively about your language.

- Don't stop speaking to your child in your language or think that he cannot progress in his ability to speak and understand your language. On the contrary, keep developing these skills and try to reinforce them.

- As a practical matter, if your child attends a weekend language school, speak with the teachers and arrange for your child to receive significantly increased help with reading and writing tasks in class and significantly decreased reading and writing homework. If the teaching staff is willing to make adjustments for children with special needs, not only can those children continue to progress in their second language, but they can do so in a way that preserves their self-esteem and motivation.

- You may also decide that under the circumstances, a weekend language school may not be the best place for your child, and that's just fine. A tutor who can work one-on-one with your child and who will focus more on speaking the language may be a better match.

- Just because the time is not right at the moment, don't assume that your child will never read and write in your language. As his reading skills in English improve, then consider slowly intensifying or reintroducing the reading process in your language.

CONCLUSION

We have now reached the end of our journey together. While I hope that this book will serve as your guidebook on *your* journey of raising your child bilingual and will be well thumbed as a result of your returning to it again and again as specific questions and issues arise, I'd like to leave you with what I believe are the three pieces of advice that I hope you will take most to heart:

1. Help your child identify positively with the language.

It's not an exaggeration to say that if your child does not identify positively with the second language, the chances of her becoming bilingual are remote. While this may sound overly dramatic, when you think about it, it makes sense. As we've discussed throughout the book, learning a second language can be fun and immensely satisfying, but there's no getting around the fact that it also requires a lot of effort and energy over a long period of time. (And as I pointed out at the beginning of Step 2, the same thing of course is true of mastering anything.) But the truth of the matter is that none of us, child or adult, is going to devote the amount of effort, energy, and time it takes to become truly proficient in a language (or at a sport or a musical instrument) unless we identify with it and feel a deep personal connection to it. Maria told me, "On the day my twin girls, who are trilingual, graduated high school, I asked them if they thought they would speak to their children in Spanish as I had done with them. They both answered yes, without hesitation. That was when I knew I had accomplished what I set out what I do. The fact that they're going to speak Spanish to their children shows me that the language is as important to them as it is to me."

2. Adjust your bilingual goals and plan as needed and let your child know you love him just as he is.

Over the many years of raising your child bilingual, at one point or another, you may find yourself in the position of needing to readjust your expectations. Remember, in many ways raising your child bilingual is no different than many other parenting goals. And as most of us parents quickly find out, parenting in general does not lend itself to goals written in stone, one-time fixes, or single solutions! The best way to deal with whatever parenting challenges lie ahead (whether related to bilingualism or not) is to try to come up with the best strategy you can for dealing with the situation at that moment, while leaving the door open for further adaptations as you go along.

Sometimes it might be necessary to scale back on your bilingual plan, and scaling back is not always an easy thing to do in our highly competitive world. You might worry that you—and your child—are giving up. I want to reassure you that nothing could be further from the truth. The last thing you want to do is to send your child the message that his best is not good enough. Not only will that cause your child to truly give up on learning a second language, but it makes it less likely that he'll want to make the effort to do his best at *anything*, and it could seriously damage your relationship with him. Adjusting your expectations when your child is having a rough time or is not progressing quite as you expected proves to your child that your love is unconditional and that you accept and love him just as he is. And a child who knows that he is supported and will not be pushed beyond what he can do is more likely to give something his all, including learning two languages.

When the tide turns, you can crank up the input again. Just try not to stop completely, though. Starting to speak your language again from scratch can be quite a challenge because it means you, the parent, will suddenly be speaking another language, something that is much less natural than simply intensifying the effort.

3. Trust the process.

On the path to bilingualism, there will be many joys as you witness your child's successful progress. Revel in them, but at the same time, don't forget about—and more importantly, don't sweat—the predictable obstacles. Your kindergartner, cruising along his developmental trajectory, might suddenly not seem so thrilled with learning your language and, for a while, might answer you back in English. Don't worry! Trust the process; this will pass.

When raising your child bilingual, you have two major forces on your side that, as long as your child identifies positively with the language, all but ensure your success: The first is your child's brain. It is ready to go and learn different languages. The second is time. Sure, learning a second (or third or fourth) language can take years, but you and your child have years in which to do it. It is never too late to start to learn a language.

People always point out to me how the forces of globalization are leading to an increased awareness of the importance of bilingualism and multiculturalism. This is true. However, as a parent, raising your child bilingual is about so much more than your child being able to speak, read, and write in two languages. It is a family adventure, a gift that you are passing on to your child, and an opportunity for him to learn about another culture and be proud of his identity.

Good luck on your journey—and enjoy it!

BILINGUAL RESOURCE LIST

Resources for Children

The Internet

> **Helpful Hints**
> - *Try out* the activities yourself first to make sure you're comfortable with them and your child will be safe online.
> - *Bookmark* your favorite activities.
> - *Integrate* them into your Bilingual Action Plan.

- **Look for Web sites that have fun activities for kids.**
  1. Search for Web sites of TV channels in your language and click on the kids' section. If the channel is devoted to children, then the Web site will be too. For example, **www.kika.de/index.shtml** is the Web site for Kinderkanal, a German TV channel for children in preschool to upper elementary grades.
  2. **www.ethnokids.net** offers educational games related to culture in French.

3. **www.dmoz.org/Kids_and_Teens** offers games and information for kids and teens in multiple languages.

4. **www.kidsolr.com** offers a full mix of activities for kids and teens. Click on the "kids of the world" icon to get to a listing of multiple countries and languages.

- **Look for Web sites that offer educational activities in a second language.**
  - **www.mathstories.com** offers math instruction in Spanish.
  - **www.syvum.fr** offers an array of educational activities in French.

- **Look for multilingual online encyclopedias.**
  - Wikipedia at **www.wikipedia.org/**
  - Dumoz at **www.dmoz.org**

- **Look for free language-learning MP3 podcasts that you can download.**
  - For example, **www.chinese pod.com**

Television

- **Consider quality children's shows that include references to other cultures and languages.**
  - *Sesame Street*
  - *Maya and Miguel*
  - *Dora the Explorer*
  - *Madeline*
  - *Dragon Tales*

- **Consider shows that are broadcast in your language.**
  - Check out foreign language channels on your cable network.
  - Visit **www.iTV.com** and **www.beelineTV.com**

Books

Check out the Skipping Stones Honor Awards, which are given to bilingual books devoted to multiculturalism (**www.skippingstones.org**).

Tapes/CDs/ DVDs

- Muzzi tapes
- Sing-along tapes
- Audiobooks
- DVDs often come in multiple languages

Materials

- Maps and globes
- Label objects around the house with their corresponding word in your language
- High-tech toys, such as Leap Frog, with foreign language materials

Fun and Games

Helpful Hints
- Kids learn through play.
- Keep in mind your child's developmental level.

Infants
- *Baby Einstein*

Toddlers
- Muzzi tapes
- Sing-along tapes in your language

Preschoolers
- Interactive, computer-based game in your language
- Sing-along tapes

School aged and adolescents
- Play family games in another language
- Play word games in the second language
- Sign up for a pen-pal (either "snail mail" or e-mail), who lives in a country where your language is spoken

Other Activities

- Visit ethnic stores and restaurants: Children can order food in another language and sample different menus

Family Members

Ask relatives to engage with your child in your language through:
- Letters
- E-mails
- Birthday cards
- Sending materials, such as games, books, articles, materials of interests for each individual child

Nonfamily Members

- Engage an au pair. For a small weekly salary, the au pair will live at your home for a year and tutor your children in her language.
- Engage bilingual babysitters. Post an ad at your local college or community bulletin board.
- Engage an at-home tutor.

Resources for Parents

Books for Parents About Raising Children Bilingual

- *Foundations of Bilingual Education and Bilingualism*, 4th edition, C. Baker (Multilingual Matters, 2006).
- *A Parents' and Teachers' Guide to Bilingualism*, 3rd edition, C. Baker (Multilingual Matters 2007).
- *The Bilingual Family: A Handbook for Parents*, E. Harding and P. Reilly (Cambridge University Press, 1987).
- *Raising Multilingual Children: Foreign Language Acquisition and Children*, T. Tokuhama-Espinosa (Bergin and Garvey, 2000).
- *One Child, Two Languages: A Guide for Preschool Educators of Children Learning English as a Second Language*, O.T. Patton (Brookes Publishing Company, 1997).

Magazines for Parents About Raising Children Bilingual

- *Bilingual Family Newsletter,* published by Multilingual Matters.

"Do-It-Yourself" Language-Learning Programs on CD-ROMS or On-line

- Examples include, but certainly are not limited to, Rosetta Stone, The Learnables, Power Glide, Transparent Language, Tell Me More.
- Check your local library (some local libraries carry one language program that patrons can access for free).

Web Sites about Raising Children Bilingual

- www.cal.org/earlylang offers bilingual resources for parents and teachers of children in grades K–8.

- **www.byu.edu/~bilingual** is specifically geared to monolingual parents. Here, monolingual parents can chat and share information with other monolingual parents who are raising bilingual children.
- **www.multilingualchildren.org** and **www.bilingaulfamiliesconnect.com**
- **www.tsl.state.tx.us/ld/projects/ninos/index.html** offers information about children's books and literacy in Spanish.

Web Sites That Offer News in Foreign Languages

- **www.kidon.com/media-link/index.php** is a great site where you can find a page for the country of your interest and a list of online TV programs, radio boradcasts, and newspapers.
- **www.cnn.co.jp/** and **www.yomiuri.co.jp** offer news in Japanese.
- **www.dw-world.de** and **www.morgenpost.de/** offer news in German.
- **www.courrierinternational.com/gabarits/html/default_online.asp** and **www.lequipe.fr/** offer news and sports respectively, in French.
- **www.elmundo.es/** offers news in Spanish.

Web Sites from Which to Purchase Foreign Language Materials

- **www.wor.com** offers books and DVDs for sale in multiple languages.
- **www.amazon.com**: Click "international sites" to buy books in different languages.
- **http://csbs.csusm.edu/csbs/www.book.book_home?lang=SP** offers books in Spanish by age and country.

Language Learning Support

- **At-home tutoring** Call local colleges and check community bulletin boards for affordable language tutors.

- **Saturday/Sunday language schools** Use the Internet or the phone book to find out if there is a school in your area that offers weekend instruction in your language.
- **Public Schools** Check with your school system's foreign language (sometimes called world languages) director or ESL director to learn about foreign language and bilingual learning opportunities in your school district.

REFERENCES

Abu-Rabia, S., Siegel LS. (2000) "Reading, syntactic, orthographic, and working memory skills of bilingual Arabic-English speaking Canadian children." *Journal of Psycholinguistic Research,* 31(6), p. 661–678.

Anderson, R.T. (2004) "Phonological acquisition in preschoolers learning a second language via immersion: A longitudinal study." *Clinical Linguistics and Phonetics,*18 (3), p. 183–210.

Avalos, AA. (2003) "Effective second-language reading transition: From learner-specific to generic instructional models." *Bilingual Research Journal,* 27(2), p. 171–205.

Baker, C. (2006) *Foundations of bilingual education and bilingualism.* 4th edition. Multilingual Matters, Clevedon, UK.

Bialystok, E. (1999) "Effects of bilingualism and biliteracy on children's emerging concepts of print." *Developmental Psychology,* 33, p. 429–440.

Bialystok, E. (2001) *Bilingualism in development: Language, literacy, & cognition.* Cambridge University Press, New York.

Bialystok, E. et al. (2004) "Bilingualism, aging, and cognitive control: Evidence from the Simon task." *Psychology and Aging,* 19(2), p. 290–303.

Briellmann, R.S. et al. (2004) "A high-field functional MRI study of quadrilingual subjects." *Brain and Language,* 89, p. 531–542.

Bruck, P. and Genesee, F. (1995) "Phonological awareness in young second language learners." *Journal of Child Language,* 22, p. 307–324.

Campbell, R. and Sais, E. (1995) "Accelerated metalinguistic phonological awareness in bilingual children." *British Journal of Developmental Psychology,* 13, p. 61–68.

Cenoz, J. and Valencia, J. (1994) "Additive trilingualism: Evidence from the Basque Country." *Applied Psycholinguistics,* 15, p. 195–207.

Cheuk, DKL., Wong, V. and Leung, GM. (2005) "Multilingual home environment and specific language impairment: A case-control study in Chinese children." *Paediatric and Perinatal Epidemiology,* 19, p. 303–314.

Clarkson, P.C. (1992) "Language and mathematics: A comparison of bilingual and monolingual students of mathematics." *Educational Studies in Mathematics,* 23(4), p. 417–429.

Conboy B.T. and Mills D.L. (2006) "Two languages, one developing brain: Event-related potentials to words in bilingual toddlers." *Developmental Science,* 9(1), F1–F11.

Dehaene, S. et al. (1997) "Anatomical variability in the cortical representation of first and second language." *NeuroReport,* 8, p. 3809–3815.

Dehaene-Lambertz, G. and Houston, D. (1998) "Language discrimination response latencies in two-month-old infants." *Language and Speech,* 41(1), p. 21–43.

Deuchar, M. and Quay, S. (1999) "Language choice in the earliest utterances: A case study with methodological implications." *Journal of Child Language,* 26, p. 461–475.

Durkin, C. (2000) "Dyslexia and bilingual children—Does recent research assist identification?" *Dyslexia,* 6, p. 248–267.

Escobedo, TH. (1983) *Early childhood bilingual education: A Hispanic perspective.* Teachers College Press, New York.

Estes, GB., Lopez-Mayhew and B., Gardner, M. (1998) "Writing in the foreign languages department." *The WAC Journal,* 9, p. 68–81.

Evans, J. et al. (2002) "Differential bilingual laterality: Mythical monster found in Wales." *Brain and Language,* 83, p. 291–299.

Everatt, J. et al. (2000) "Dyslexia screening measures and bilingualism." *Dyslexia*, 6, p. 42–56.

Fabbro, F. (2001) "The bilingual brain: Cerebral representation of languages." *Brain and Language*, 79, p. 211–222.

Frederickson, N. and Nicolson, R. (1998) "Identifying dyslexia in bilingual children: A phonological approach with Inner London Sylheti speakers." *Dyslexia*, 4, p. 119–131.

Glennen, S. (2002) "Language development and delay in internationally adopted infants and toddlers: A review." *American Journal of Speech-Language Pathology*, 11, p. 333–339.

Gomez, C. and Reason, R. (2002) "Cross-linguistic transfer of phonological skills: A Malaysian perspective." *Dyslexia*, 8, p. 22–33.

Goodz, N. (1989) "Parental language mixing in bilingual families." *Infant Mental Health Journal*, 10, p. 25–44.

Gopaul-McNicol, S. and Thomas-Presswood, T. (1998) *Working with linguistically and culturally different children. Innovative clinical and educational approaches.* Prentice Hall, Englewood Cliffs, NJ.

Hammer, CS. et al. (2004) "Speech-language pathologists' training and confidence in serving Spanish-English bilingual children." *Journal of Communication Disorders*, 37, p. 91–108.

Haritos, C. and Hunter, C. (2003) "Listening, remembering, and speaking in two languages: How did you do that?" *Bilingual Research Journal*, 27(1), p. 73–99.

Holm, A. and Dodd, B. (2001) "Comparison of cross-language generalization following speech therapy." *Folia Phoniatrica et Logopaedica*, 53 (3), p. 166–172.

Iles, J., et al. (1999) "Convergent cortical representation of semantic processing in bilinguals." *Brain and Language*, 70, p. 347–363.

Jeffers, Susan (1988) *Feel the Fear and Do It Anyway.* Ballatine Books, New York.

Juan-Garau, M. and Perez-Vidal, C. (2001) "Mixing and pragmatic parental strategies in early bilingual acquisition." *Journal of Child Language*, 28, p. 59–86.

Kim, K., et al. (1997) "Distinct cortical areas associated with native and second languages." *Nature,* 388, p. 171–174.

Koenig, M.A. and Echols, C.H. (2003) "Infants' understanding of false labeling events: The referential role of words and the people who use them." *Cognition,* 87, p. 179–208.

Kormi-Nouri, R. et al. (2003) "Episodic and semantic memory in bilingual and monolingual children." *Scandinavian Journal of Psychology,* 44(1), p. 47–54.

Krashen, S. (1993) *The power of reading: Insights from the research.* Libraries Unlimited, Englewood, CO.

Krashen, SD. (1988) *Inquiries and insights.* Alemany Press, Haywood, CA.

Krashen, SD. (2002) "Is all-English best? A response to Bengtson." *TESOL Matters,* 12(3), 5.

Krashen, SD. (2002) "Does transition really happen? Some case histories." *The Multilingual Educator,* 3(1), 50–54.

Lasagabaster, D. (1998) "The threshold hypothesis applied to three languages in contact at school." *International Journal of Bilingual Education and Bilingualism,* 1, p. 119–133.

Lee, P. (1996) "Cognitive development in bilingual children: A case for bilingual instruction in early childhood education." *Bilingual Research Journal,* 20(3–4), p. 499–522.

Lesaux, NK. and Siegel, LS. (2003) "The development of reading in children who speak English as a second language." *Developmental Psychology,* 39(6), p. 1005–1019.

Limbos, MM. and Geva, E. (2001) "Accuracy of teacher assessments of second-language students at risk for reading disability." *Journal of Learning Disabilities,* 34(2), p. 136–151.

Lindholm-Leary, KJ. and Borsato, G. (2001) "Impact of two-way bilingual elementary programs on students' attitudes toward school and college." *Center for research on education, diversity & excellence.* University of California, Berkeley.

Marchman, V.A. and Martinez-Sussmann, C. and Dale, P.S. (2004) "The language-specific nature of grammatical development: Evidence from bilingual language learners." *Developmental Science,* 7, p. 212–224.

McBride-Chang, C. et al. (2004) "Levels of phonological awareness in three cultures." *Journal of Experimental Child Psychology,* 89(2), p. 93–111.

Montague, N. (1995) "The process oriented approach to teaching writing to second language learners." *New York State Association for Bilingual Education Journal,* 10, p. 13–24.

Moore, C., Angelopoulos, M. and Benette, P. (1999) "Word learning in the context of referential and salience cues." *Developmental Psychology,* 35 (1), p. 60–68.

Nagai, P.B. (2002) "Bilingual education for all: A benefits model for small towns." *Bilingual Research Journal,* 26 (2), p. 269–294.

O'Toole, S. et al. (2001) "Development of reading proficiency in English by bilingual children and their monolingual peers." *Psychological Reports,* 89(2), p. 279–282.

Ojemann, G.A. (1983) "Brain organization for language from the perspective of electrical stimulation mapping." *The Behavioral and Brain Sciences,* 2, p. 189–207.

Oketani, H. (1997) "Additive bilinguals: The case of post-war second generation Japanese Canadian youths." *Bilingual Research Journal,* 21(4), p. 359–379.

Paradis, J. and Crago, M. (2000) "Tense and temporality: A comparison between children and learning a second language and children with SLI." *Journal of Speech, Language, and Hearing Research,* 43, p. 834–847.

Paradis, J. et al. (2003) "French-English bilingual children with SLI: How do they compare with their monolingual peers?" *American Speech-Language-Hearing Association,* 46, p. 113–127.

Paradis, J. and Navarro, S. (2003) "Subject realization and crosslinguistic interference in the bilingual acquisition of Spanish and English: What is the role of the input?" *Journal of Child Language,* 30, p. 371–393.

Patterson, J. (1998) "Expressive vocabulary development and word combinations of Spanish-English bilingual toddlers." *American Journal of Speech-Language Pathology,* 7, p. 45–56.

Peal, E. and Lambert, W. (1962) "The relation of bilingualism to intelligence." *Psychological Monographs,* 76, p. 1–23.

Pearson, B.Z. and Fernandez, M. (1994) "Patterns of interaction in the lexical development in two languages of bilingual infants." *Language Learning,* 44, p. 617–653.

Pearson, B.Z., Fernandez, M. and Oller, D.K. (1993) "Lexical development in bilingual infants and toddlers: Comparison to monolingual norms." *Language Learning,* 43, p. 93–120.

Pena, E., Bedore, L. and Zlatic-Giunta, R. (2002) "Category-generation performance of bilingual children: The influence of condition, category, and language." *Journal of Speech, Language, and Hearing Research,* 45, p. 938–947.

Perani, D., et al. (1998) "The bilingual brain: Proficiency and age of acquisition of the second language." *Brain,* 121, p. 1841–1852.

Perozzi, J.A. and Chavez Sanchez, M.L. (1992) "The effect of Instruction in L1 on receptive acquisition of L2 for bilingual children with language delay." *Language, Speech and Hearing Services in Schools,* 23, p. 248–352.

Portes, A. and Hao, L. (2002) "The price of uniformity: Language, family, and personality adjustment in the immigrant second generation." *Ethnic and Racial Studies,* 25, p. 889–912.

Rafferty, E.A. (1986) "Second language study and basic skills in Louisiana." *Office of Research and Development.* Louisiana State Department of Education, Baton Rouge, LA.

Ray, J. (2002) "Treating phonological disorders in a multilingual child: A case study." *American Journal of Speech-Language Pathology,* 11, p. 305–315.

Rice, M.L. and Woodsmall, L. (1988) "Lessons from television: Children's word learning when viewing." *Child Development,* 59, p. 420–429.

Rice, M.L. et al. (1990) "Words from 'Sesame Street': Learning vocabulary while viewing." *Developmental Psychology,* 26, p. 421–428.

Ridge, M. (1981) *The new bilingualism: An American dilemma.* Center for Study of the American Experience, Los Angeles.

Rioux, F.E., et al. (2004) "Intra-operative mapping of cortical areas involved in reading in mono- and bilingual patients." *Brain*, 127, p. 1796–1810.

Ruan, J. (2003) "A study of bilingual Chinese/English children's code switching behavior." *Academic Exchange Quarterly*, 7, Iss. 1.

Sanz, C. (2000) "Bilingual education enhances third language acquisition: Evidence from Catalonia." *Applied Psycholinguistics*, 21, p. 23–44.

Scovel, T. (2000). "A critical review of the critical period research." *Annual Review of Applied Linguistics*, 20, p. 213–223.

Soto, L.D. (2002) "Young bilingual children's perceptions of bilingualism and biliteracy: Altruistic possibilities." *Bilingual Research Journal*, 26(3), p. 599–610.

Swain, M. and Lapkin, S. (1989) "Canadian immersion and adult second language teaching: What's the connection?" *Modern Language Journal*, 73(2), p. 150–159.

Swain, M., Lapkin, S. and Rowen, N. (1990) "The role of mother tongue literacy in third language learning." *Language, Culture, and Curriculum*, 3(1), p. 65–81.

Tokuhama-Espinosa, T. (2000) *Raising multilingual children: Foreign language acquisition and children.* Bergin and Garvey, Westport, Connecticut.

Toppelberg, CO., Snow, CE. and Tager-Flusberg, H. (1999) "Severe developmental disorders and bilingualism." *Journal of the American Academy of Child and Adolescent Psychiatry*, 38(9), p. 1197–1199.

Weikum. W.M et al. (2007) "Visual language discrimination in infancy." *Science*, 316, p. 1159.

Worthy, J., Rodriguez-Galindo, A. (2003) "Fifth-grade bilingual students and precursors to 'subtractive schooling.'" *Bilingual Research Journal*, 27(2), p. 275–294.

Wu, T., Kansaku, K. and Hallett, M. (2004) "How self-initiated memorized movements become automatic: A fMRI study." *Journal of Neurophysiology*, 91(4), p. 1690–1698.

Yelland, G. W., Pollard, J. and Mercuri, A. (1993) "The metalinguistic benefits of limited contact with a second language." *Applied Psycholinguistics,* 14(4), p. 423–444.

Yuuko, U. (2005) "Narrative development in bilingual kindergartners: Can Arthur help?" *Developmental Psychology,* 41(3), p. 464–478.

INDEX

A

Academic performance, effect of bilingualism on, 20–21

Activities, for language input/language learning, 55–56, 66, 73, 103, 126

choosing your own, 93, 94–96

"old-fashioned," 73–74

scheduling of, 93, 97

technology-based, 67–72

computer games, 70–71

computers and the Internet, 67–70, 150, 175–176

interactive educational toys, 71

radio, 68, 72

television, 68–69, 71–72, 176

videos and DVDs, 72

Adolescents

bilingualism acquisition in, 10–11

as second-generation immigrants, 22

Adults

bilingualism acquisition in, 10–11

language-learning ability of, 30–31

Advanced Placement (AP), 81, 163

Age factors. *See also* Adolescents; Adults

in bilingualism, 9–11, 18

Algeria, bilingualism in, 4

Alliance Française, 90

American Academy of Pediatrics

Internet safety guidelines of, 150

television/video-watching guidelines of, 67

Anxiety, affecting expression in a second language, 43–44

Arabic language, 4

Arthur (television program), 71–72

B

Babysitters, role in Bilingual Action Plan, 75–76, 78

Balanced bilinguals, 3, 6, 15, 45, 46, 116

Basque language, 4

Between the Lions (television program), 71

Bilingual Action Plan, 65–97

changing of, *see* modification of

creating your own, 93–97

examples of, 84–93

monolingual family, 88–90

One-Parent-One-Language (OPOL), 90–93

One-Parent-One-Language (OPOL) with variations, 85–87

Bilingual Action Plan (*continued*)
  maintenance of consistency in, 57–58
  maximization of language input at home
      component, 65, 66–74
    with "old-fashioned" activities,
        73–74
    with technology-based activities, 67–72
  modification of, 125–127, 163–169,
      172–173
  other parent's support, importance of, 123
  periodic revision of, 84
  school support component, 78–84
    at-home tutoring, 82–83
    "do-it-yourself" language-learning
        programs, 83
    foreign-language summer camps,
        83–84
    public schools, 80–81, 153–154,
        155–153
    reasons for, 78–80
    Saturday or Sunday language schools,
        81, 90, 92
  utilization of community and family
      resources component, 74–78
    babysitters, 75–76, 78
    creation of, 78
    extended family, 76–77
    friends and neighbors, 74
    local library, 75
    travel, 77–78
  Weekly, 84, 86, 89, 91
Bilingual families, 1–2
Bilingual education programs in the United
    States
  dual immersion programs, 158
  history of, 155
  ESL or English as a second language, 158
  important information for parents, 160
  transitional education programs, 156
  two-way or dual immersion programs,
      158

Bilingualism
  adding a third language in, 37
  advantages and benefits of, 2, 19–24
    academic benefits, 20–21
    in family and community, 22–24
    language benefits, 19
    other cognitive benefits, 21–22
  balanced, 3, 6, 15, 45, 46, 116
  choice of languages for, 27–28, 32–40
    common questions about, 33–39
  common myths about, *see* Myths about
      bilingualism
  components of, 3
  definition of, 2–3
  maintenance of, 36–37
  mixing as a normal stage in, 6–9
  motivations for, 1–2, 31–32, 78–79
  parents' ambivalence about, 31–32, 52–53,
      55
  passive, 15–16, 18, 45–46
  postponement of, 27, 42, 125, 127
  as priority, 52–54
  unequal language proficiency in, 3, 6
Bilingual parents
  motivation for child's bilingualism, 31–32
  obstacles to child's bilingualism, 31–32
Bilingual Public Charter School,
      Washington, D. C., 161
Bilinguals Act of 1968, 156
Books
  bilingual books, 140
  choosing difficulty level of, 134
  cultural references in, 133
  interactive, 135
  picture books, 136
    with accompanying CDs, 73
  selection of, 134–135, 136
Brain development, role in language
      acquisition and bilingualism, 4–6
  adaptation to language environment, 9
  age factors affecting, 9–11

as "bilingual" brain, advantages of, 21–22

dominant language use, 47–48, 108–109

language acquisition process in, 6–7

multiple language acquisition, 37

plasticity effect in, 5, 47

in simultaneous bilingualism, 40

surges and plateaus in, 100

"use it or lose it" effect in, 36

Boxes, *see* Tip boxes

C

Canada, passive bilingualism in, 16

Caregivers, role in children's bilingualism, 60

Cassettes, sing-along, 73

Catalan language, 4

CDs

use in language input/language
    acquisition, 73, 83

use in reading skill development, 135

Center for Applied Linguistics, 80

Cheaper by the Dozen (film), 54

Child development. *See also* Developmental
    delays; Brain development

sporadic nature of, 100

Children's books, *see* Books

Children with special needs being raised
    bilingual

linguistically talented, 165

talented, 164–165

with developmental delays, 165–168

with reading and writing difficulties,
    168–169

Chinese-American students, 156

Chinese language

free podcasts in, 70

Mandarin Chinese, 15, 25–26, 70, 85–87

Civil Rights Act of 1964, 156

Choice of language, *see* Language choice

Coaches, bilingual, 51–63

language boundaries approach of, 61–63

major tasks of

ensuring correct amount of language
    input, 54

making bilingualism a priority,
    52–54

teaching, 54–56

One-Parent-One-Language (OPOL)

strategy of, 56–61

variations on, 60–61

parent as a, 51, 54–56

use of family activities by, 74

Code switching, 115–116, 117

Cognitive development, role of language in,
    21

College students, as foreign language tutors,
    82–83

Communication skills. *See also* Reading;
    Writing; Language as
    communication

bilingualism-related, 22, 23

Community resources, as Bilingualism
    Action Plan component, 75–78

Compound words, creation of, 8

Computer-based language-learning
    programs, 83

Computer games, 70–71

Computers, 67–68

Conflict, parent-child, bilingualism as
    source of, 110–113

Consistency, in bilingualism, 108–109

with children with developmental delays,
    167

in language input, 108–109

in One-Parent-One-Language (OPOL)
    strategy, 57–58

Cuban immigrants, 155

Cultural factors, in bilingualism, 22–24,
    112

D

Darja language, 4

Deutsche Sonnabendschule, 161

Developmental delays, in language
acquisition, 11–14, 18, 165–168
Developmental factors, in resistance to
bilingualism, 109–110
Developmental screening tests, 13
Dialects, 33
"Do-It-Yourself" Language-learning
programs, 83
Dominant language, 47–48
parents' lack of proficiency in, 34–35
second language becomes, 101–102
Dora the Explorer (television program), 69,
153
Dragon Tales (television program), 153
Drawing, role in writing process, 144, 146,
148
Drills, use in language learning, 105
Dual immersion programs, 158–161
Dutch language, 4
Dyslexia, 168

E
Elementary and Secondary Education Act of
1965, 156
Elementary schools, foreign language
instruction in, 80–81, 137–139, 162
Embarrassment, bilingualism as source of,
53, 110–111
Encouragement, 106
English as Second Language (ESL)
programs, 154, 155, 158, 160
English language. *See also* Dominant
language
children's preference for, 107–113
German and French roots of, 20
as official language of the United States,
17, 18
worldwide prevalence of, 16–18
Environment. *See* Language environment
Extended family, role in Bilingual Action
Plan, 76–77

F
Family heritage, language as link to. *See*
Heritage languages
Family resources, as Bilingualism Action
Plan component, 75–78
Feel the Fear and Do It Anyway (Jeffers), 121
FLEX ("Foreign Language Exploratory/
Experience") programs, 162
Foreign countries, children's acquisition of
bilingualism in, 93, 77–78, 36–37
"Foreign Language Exploratory/Experience"
(FLEX) programs, 162
Friends, role in Bilingual Action Plan, 74

G
Game Boy, 70–71
Genetic factors, in language acquisition, 5
German language, 151–152
Gestures, 103, 104
Gifted child, *see* Talented child
Globalization, 24, 30, 173
Goals, in bilingualism, 16, 25–50
defining of, 25–50
choice of language, 27–28, 29, 32–40
identification of motivations for, 28,
30–32
sequential bilingualism, 40, 41–42
setting a start date for bilingualism,
40–43
simultaneous bilingualism, 40–41, 42
"to-do" list for, 27
discussion with child of, 53–54
realistic, 46–47
revision of, 126, 172–173
time factors, and hectic schedule, 58
worksheet for, 49–50
Goldilocks and the Three Bears, 146
Grammar rules and skills, 8, 142, 143, 147,
151
Grandparents, role in Bilingual Action Plan,
76–77, 85, 87

H

Hebrew language, 8

Heritage languages, 22, 24
   children's positive identification with,
      171–172, 173
   children's refusal to speak, 107–113
   value and benefits of, 33–35

High schools, foreign-language study in,
   161–162

High-school students, language skill transfer
   in, 41–42

Hindi language, 5

Holland, bilingualism in, 4

Home-schooling, 82

I

Identity, sense of, 22–23

Identification with heritage language, *see*
      Heritage language

Idioms, 142

Immersion programs, 158–161

Immigrant children
   lack of bilingual education for, 155–156

Immigrants, English language proficiency of,
   16–17

Indian immigrants, languages spoken
      among, 33

Individualized approach for children with
      special needs, *see* Child with special
      needs

Infants
   bilingualism ability and development in,
      4–5, 9
   preference for native language, 5

Intelligence, relationship to bilingualism,
   4–6, 18, 21–22, 23

Intelligence quotient (IQ) testing, 21–22

Internet, 68–70

J

Journals, 151

K

Kids Online Resources web site, 69

Kindergarten children, pre-reading skill
   development in, 134

L

Labels, use in reading skills development,
   138–139

Language. *See also specific languages*
   as communication, 8, 22, 23
   emotional attachment to, 27–28
   values and benefits of, 33–35

Language acquisition
   in adults, 30–31
   developmental delays in, 11–14, 18,
      165–168
   genetic factors in, 5
   in infants, 4–5
   of multiple languages, 37
   range of "normal" in, 12
   role of reading in, 129
   speed of, 58
   surge and plateaus in, 100–101

Language boundaries, 61–63, 66

Language choice,
   six most common questions about, 27–38
   more than two languages, 37
   multilingual families, 37
   my language is not an "important"
      language, 33
   parent does not speak second language
      fluently, 35
   parent is not fluent in native language,
      34
   picking up a language in a foreign
      country, 36
   which languages are important to you,
      27

Language delay, 18, 165–166
   expressive, 12, 166
   temporary, 11

Language environment
  brain's adaptation to, 9
  effect on language acquisition, 11
  role in Bilingual Action Plan, 8
Language input
  complexity of, 46
  consistency in, 108–109
  effect on language acquisition, 102, 104
  parents' role in, 35
  required for language proficiency, 46
  tips for maximization of, 103–104
Language lag, 166
  expressive, 12, 166
Language milestones in bilingual children,
    12
Language mixing
  differentiated from
    code switching, 115–116
    translation, 105
  as obstacle to bilingualism, 113–118
  parents' management of, 116–118
Language proficiency
  alleged adverse effect of bilingualism on,
    6–9
  effect of language stimulation on,
    15–16
  language input required for, 46
  in multiple languages, 38
  realistic goals in, 46–47
  role of stimulation in, 5–6, 15–16
  unequal, 3, 6
  writing-based development of, 142
Language Questionnaire (Worksheet 1), 28,
    29, 38
Language skills, higher-level, 35, 41–42
Language schools, *see* Saturday or Sunday
    schools
Language therapists, *see* Speech and
    language therapist
Late-talker, 167
Lau vs. Nichols, 156

Learnables, The (language learning
    program), 83
Lessing, Doris, 149
Letter-sound recognition, 132
Libraries, role in Bilingual Action Plan, 75
Linguistic talent, 165
Listening, active, 106

M
Madeline (television program), 153
Mandarin Chinese, 15, 25–26, 85–87
  free podcasts in, 70
Martin, Steve, 54
Maya and Miguel (television program),
    153
Middle-school students, language skill
    transfer in, 41–42
Monolingual children, vocabulary of, 12
Monolingual parents, 23
  of bilingual children, 14–15
  case examples of, 25–26
  motivation for child's bilingualism, 28,
    29–31
  obstacles to child's bilingualism faced by,
    30
Motivation, for bilingualism, 1–2, 28–32,
    78–79
MP3 podcasts, 70
Multiculturalism, 112, 173
Multilingual families, One-Parent-One-
    Language (OPOL) use with, 59–60
Multilingualim, 37–38
My Bilingual Goals and Choice Worksheet,
    49–50
Myths about bilingualism, 4–18
  myth 1: Only intelligent children can be
    bilingual, 4–6
  myth 2: Bilingualism leads to confusion,
    6–9
  myth 3: Children can't learn a language
    after age five, 9–11

myth 4: Bilingualism leads to language delay, 11–14

myth 5: Monolingual parents can't raise a bilingual child, 14–15

myth 6: Children absorb languages passively, 15–16

myth 7: English language is losing ground, 17–18

N

National Survey of Foreign Language Instruction in the United States, 80

Native languages. *See* Heritage languages

Neighbors, role in Bilingual Action Plan, 74

Normans, 20

Nursery rhymes, 35, 73

O

Obstacles, to bilingualism, 99–127

anxiety, 43–44, 110

children's preference for the English language, 107–113

faced by monolingual parents, 30

language mixing, 105, 113–118

parents' self-consciousness, 119–122

parents' uncertainty, 99, 100–107

parents' work schedule, 125, 127

shyness, 43–44

unequal parental involvement in, 122–125

One-Parent-One-Language (OPOL) strategy, 56–61, 90–93, 119

consistency in, 57–58

definition of, 56

obstacle to, 60

variations on, 60–61

Oral language skills, 129–130

P

Paraphrasing, 107

Parents. *See also* Bilingual parents; Monolingual parents

ambivalence toward children's bilingualism, 31–32, 52–53, 55

as bilingualism coaches. *See* Coaches, bilingual

interaction with other parents, 70

multilingual, 37–38

necessity of both parents' involvement in child's bilingualism, 122–125

as role models for bilingualism, 10–11, 15

self-consciousness in speaking your language in public, 119–122

unequal involvement in child's bilingualism, 122–125

Passive bilingualism, 15–16, 18, 45–46

PBS (Public Broadcasting Station), 71–72

Pen pals, 92, 150

Phonemes, 132

Phonetic rules, in writing, 144, 145

Phonics, 131, 134

Phonological awareness, 20–21

Picture books, 136

with accompanying CDs, 73

Play groups, 78

PlayStation, 70–71

Podcasts, 70

Poetry, 35

Pointing, 103, 104

Power Glide (language learning program), 83

Predictable obstacles, 99–127

predictable obstacle 1: You're not sure you're speaking to your child in a way that will help him become bilingual, 100–107

predictable obstacle 2: Your child wants to speak only English, 107–113

predictable obstacle 3: Your child keeps mixing languages, 113–118

predictable obstacle 4: You're self-conscious about speaking your language in public, 119–125

Predictable obstacles (*continued*)
    predictable obstacle 5: Because you're the
      parent who speaks the language, you
      feel like you're doing all the work
      raising your child bilingual, 122–125
    predictable obstacle 6: Your work schedule
      allows little time for bilingualism,
      125–127
Pre-reading skills, 132, 134
Preschool children, pre-reading skill
    development in, 134
Prewriting skills, 144, 148
Pride, bilingualism as source of, 53, 110–111
Problem solving, bilinguals better at, 21–22,
    23
Puberty. *See also* Adolescents
    language acquisition after, 9
Public schools, foreign language/bilingual
      education programs in, 80–81,
      153–154, 155–163
    advanced placement in, 81, 163
    as bilingual schools, 161
    as English as Second Language (ESL)
      programs, 154, 155, 158, 160
    5 things to know about, 160–163
    foreign-language departments and, 160, 162
    history of, 155–156
    limited choice of languages offered, 162
    multicultural, multilingual activities in,
      39–40
    sequencing issue in, 162–163
    short-term progress in, 39–40
    transitional programs, 156–159
    two-way, or dual, immersion programs,
      158–161

Q
Question-asking, 106
Q&As
    continuing to read to a child who can
      read on her own, 135

    correcting your child's writing, 143
    effects of limited language input on
      language acquisition, 58
    handling teacher concerns about mistakes
      children make while learning to
      write in two languages, 151
    passive learning of a second language, 45
    self-taught reading in a second language,
      133
    short-term school second-language
      programs, 39
    speaking a new language in new
      environment, 43
    switching languages will not speed up
      language development, 102
    translating words to aid comprehension,
      104
    usefulness of teaching body parts or other
      language drills, 105

R
Radiotelevisione Italiana, 68
Reading, in a second language, 20–21, 102,
      129–141. *See also* books
    advantages of, 129–131
    develops and safeguards language skills,
      131
    different kind of language exposure,
      130
    higher level language skills, 130
    increased cognitive benefits, 130
    increased vocabulary and better
      understanding, 130
    strengthens preexisting speaking skills,
      129–130
    adults' proficiency in, 30
    advanced skill levels in, 47
    books, choosing level of difficulty, 134
    children who teach themselves to read in
      a second language, 133
    cognitive basis for, 131–132

cognitive benefits of, 130–131
difficulty in, 168–169
encouraging children to become life-long
 readers in your language, 138
effect on language proficiency, 130
effect on lifelong maintenance of
 bilingualism, 131
home curricula for, 137
language skill transfer in, 133–134
pre-reading skills in, 132, 134
in preschool/kindergarten, 73, 134–137,
 139
oral understanding as a support of,
 129–130
proficiency in, 45, 164–165
pronunciation in, 131–132
reading in a second language is more
 tiring, 133, 138
reading rules for, 137
relationship to speaking skills, 129–130
as source of higher-level language skills,
 130
in upper elementary grades, 139–141
 at-home reading requirements and,
 139–140
use of flash cards in, 138
use of labels in, 138–139
vocabulary acquisition in, 130, 132–133,
 135, 136, 137
Reading and writing difficulties, 168–169
Reading specialists, 168
Repetition, 104
Resources, for bilingualism, 65, 175–181
 for children, 175–178
 for parents, 179–181
Rhymes and rhyming, 35, 73, 134
Role models, in bilingualism, 10–11, 15
Romance languages, 20
Rosetta Stone (language-learning program),
 83
Russian language, 5

S
Scheduling
 of activities for language input/language
 learning, 93, 97
 for bilingualism instruction, 54
Schools. See also Elementary schools; High
 schools; Public schools
 as component of Bilingual Action Plan,
 78–84
 at-home tutoring, 82–83
 "do-it-yourself" language-learning
 programs, 83
 foreign-language summer camps,
 83–84
 public schools, 80–81, 153–154,
 155–163
 reasons for, 78–80
 Saturday or Sunday language schools,
 81, 90, 92, 161, 169
 foreign, English language use in, 36
 language instruction in
 multicultural, multilingual activities
 in, 39–40
 short-term progress in, 39–40
 private bilingual, 153–154
Second languages
 children's exposure to, 35–37
 parents' acquisition of, 35–36
 parents' lack of fluency in, 35–36
Sequential bilingualism, 40, 41, 42–44
Sesame Street (television program), 69, 71,
 153
Shyness,
 affecting expression in second language,
 43–44
"Silent period," 43–44
Simultaneous bilingualism, 40, 42
Songs and singing, 73
Spain, bilingualism in, 4
Spanish language, infants' recognition
 of, 5

Speaking skills, relationship to reading skills, 130

Speech and language assessment, 13, 41, 166

Speech and language pathologists/therapists, 13, 41, 165–166

Speech development, bilingualism-related delay in, 11

Spelling rules, 142, 143, 146, 151

Start date, 40

Stimulation, role in language proficiency, 5–6, 15–16

Storytelling, 35, 150

Summer camps, with language instruction programs, 83–84

Support system, bilingual, 126

T

Talented child, 164–165

Talking, age of onset of, 40, 165–166
developmental delays in, 40–41, 166–167

Teachers
attitudes toward bilingualism, 13
parents as, 54–56

Technology-based activities, for language input/language learning, 67–72
computer games, 70–71
computers and the Internet, 67–70, 150, 175–176
interactive educational toys, 71
radio, 68, 72
television, 68–69, 71–72, 176
videos and DVDs, 72

Teletubbyland (video), 72

Tell Me More (language learning program), 83

Temperament, role in learning a second language, 163

Thinking
abstract, 21
analytical, 20

effect of bilingualism on, 131
effect of language skills on, 35

Time factors/timing, in
bilingualism/language acquisition, 40–42, 46–47
for children with speech and language delay, 167

Tips
Dos and Don'ts for Handling Language Mixing, 118
Examples of Language Boundaries, 61
Reasons Why One-Parent-One-Language is Such a Successful Way to Raise a Bilingual Child, 57
Things to Do When Your Child Is Not Speaking Your Language, 109
Things to Remember When Choosing a Second Language for Your Child, 39
Things You Can Do Now to Encourage Your Child to Become a Life-Long Reader in Your Language, 138–139
Things That Can Help You Continue on to Path to Bilingualism—Even When it Feels Like You Can't, 126
Things You Can Do to Make Speaking Another Language in Public Easier, 121
Tips for Encouraging Your Child to Chat, 106
Tips to Make Sequential Bilingualism Easier, 43
Tips for Speaking/Interacting With Your Child to Achieve Maximum Language Input, 103–104
Tricks of the Trade for Reading to Your Child in Your Language, 136
Troubleshooting Guide: 7 Frequent Situations and Where to Find Solutions in This Book, 55

Ways to Encourage Your Child to Write in Your Language, 149–151
Ways to Ensure That Your "Non-Speaking" Partner Is Actively Involved in Raising Your Child Bilingual, 125
Ways to Help Your Preschooler or Kindergartner Feel Good about Speaking Your Language, 111
Why Technology is Such a Strong Second Language Partner, 67
Toddlers, vocabulary "surge" in, 100
Toys, interactive educational, 71
Transfer, of language skills, 41, 101–102, 132, 157
    in children with speech and language delay, 167
    through reading, 133–134
Transitional bilingual programs, 156–157
Translation, 7, 104–105
Transparent Language (language learning program). 83
Travel
    bilingual goals during, 93
    role in Bilingual Action Plan, 77–78
Troubleshooting guide, for bilingualism, 55
Tutoring, in languages, at-home, 82–83
Two-way (dual), immersion programs, 158–161

U
"Use it or lose it" effect, 36

V
Vocabulary, of bilingual children, 11–12, 40
    reading-related increase in, 130, 132–133, 135, 136, 137
    "surge" in acquisition of, 100, 101
    writing-based acquisition of, 146, 148
    writing-based reinforcement of, 141–142

W
Wikipedia, 66, 70
Weekend language schools, *see* Saturday or Sunday schools
Worksheets,
    worksheet 1: Language Questionnaire, 29
    worksheet 2: Step 2 Wrap-up: My Bilingual Goals and Choices, 49
    worksheet 3: What Are the Key Components to My Bilingual Action Plan, 94–96
    worksheet 4: Our Family's Weekly Bilingual Schedule, 97
Word banks, 141–142, 149
World of Reading Web site, 68
World Wide Web, 68
"Writer's block," 146
Writing, in a second language, 45, 102, 141–152
    advantages of
        acquisition of grammar skills, 142
        development of higher-level language skills, 142
        improvement of spoken language skills, 143
        more nuanced understanding of the language, 142
        reinforcement of vocabulary, 141–142
    comparison with writing in a dominant language, 148
    difficulty in, 168
    encouraging children in, 149–151
    grammar rules in, 142, 143, 147, 151
    parents' corrections of, 143
    skill levels in, 143–148
        advanced level, 47, 148
        intermediate level, 147
        prewriting, 144
        writing sentences, 145–146

Writing, in a second language (*continued*)
  writing short paragraphs (beginner's
    level), 146–147
  writing words, 144–145
spelling rules in, 142, 143, 146, 151
topics to write about, 149–150

X

Xbox, 71

Z

Zulu language, 5